FUCKING
INNOCENT

THE EARLY FILMS OF
WES ANDERSON

John Andrew Fredrick

FUCKING
INNOCENT

THE EARLY FILMS OF
WES ANDERSON

Rare Bird Books | Los Angeles, Calif.

A Rare Bird Book | Rare Bird Books
453 South Spring Street, Suite 302
Los Angeles, CA 90013
rarebirdbooks.com

FIRST TRADE PAPERBACK ORIGINAL EDITION

Set in Dante
Printed in the United States

10 9 8 7 6 5 4 3 2 1

Publisher's Cataloging-in-Publication data
Names: Fredrick, John Andrew, author.
Title: Fucking innocent , the early films of Wes Anderson / John Andrew Fredrick.
Description: First Trade Paperback Original Edition | A Genuine Rare Bird Book |
New York, NY; Los Angeles, CA: Rare Bird Books, 2017.
Identifiers: ISBN 9781945572555
Subjects: LCSH Anderson, Wes, 1969—Criticism and interpretation. | Motion
picture producers and directors—United States. | BISAC PERFORMING ARTS /
Film / Direction & Production | PERFORMING ARTS / Individual Director.
Classification: LCC PN1998.3.A526 F74 2017 | DDC 791.4302/33—dc23

The study of myself for its own sake, the comprehension of that attention itself and the desire to trace clearly for myself the nature of my own existence, almost never abandoned me. This secret disease alienates one from letters, despite the fact that it has its source in them.

—Paul Valery

I have a way of filming things and staging them and designing sets. There were times when I thought I should change my approach, but in fact, this is what I like to do. It's sort of like my handwriting as a movie director. And somewhere along the way, I think I've made my decision: I'm going to write in my own handwriting...I chose philosophy [as a major in college] because it sounded like something I ought to be interested in. What I really spent my time doing was writing short stories—what I really wanted to do was make stories one way or another...I've always wanted to work in theater. I feel like theater is a big part of my movie work. —Wes Anderson

To be is to be perceived. —Bishop Berkeley

The brave man is he who overcomes not only his enemies but his pleasures. —Democritus

A director only makes one movie in his life. Then he breaks it into pieces and he makes it again. —Jean Renoir

CONTENTS

ONE *Bottle Rocket (Saving)* **1**

TWO *Rushmore (Acting)* **65**

THREE *The Royal Tenenbaums (Being)* **119**

To all the Dignans, Anthonys, Mr. Blumes, Miss Crosses, Maxes, Berts, Mr. LittleJeans, Margarets, Dr. Guggenheims, Royals, Margots, "Baumers," Ethelines, Henry Shermans, Pagodas, and Raleigh St. Clairs— "You may say I'm a dreamer but I'm not the only one."

—John Winston Lennon

For John Chandler Fredrick

ONE

Bottle Rocket (Saving)

Hey, Anthony—don't try to save everybody, okay?!

—Dr. Nichols

Roland, Hamlet, Heathcliff, Romeo, Dignan. Dignan? That Anderson's given his co-hero/foil the single-handle treatment is revealing on several levels. Is Dignan Dignan's Christian or surname? Does it matter? Dignan's ambiguous moniker adds to his ostensible mystery and stature, surely, à la the aforementioned titans from literature; it signals moreover that he must be larger-than-life, like a character in a film—or that he fancies he is, at least, which, as Dignan is self-absorption personified, is, to him, just as good as being the real deal. *Bottle Rocket*, first in the putative trilogy of important, beautifully shot, self-reflexive films that establishes Wes Anderson as a promising then masterly auteur, is a movie about the movies.

As is *Rushmore*. As is, to a lesser but nevertheless significant extent, *The Royal Tenenbaums*. In a cinematic world that churns out romantic tripe and concatenations of explosions set to hiccupping soundtracks in punishingly loud and egregious Sensurround, *Bottle Rocket* is that rare thing: a film about friendship—and that's its main theme. It's a morality play and psychodrama. It's also about Peter Pan syndrome, and two characters who are, as Dignan declares, "fucking innocent." *Bottle Rocket* examines the American Dream (or Scam), and is greatly concerned with philosophy, charity, and saintliness in particular: which is why, I am going to argue, Anderson calls the other hero Anthony, the patron saint of lost and stolen things, and of lost souls. Moreover, the film is about love— and the lack of it, and the immortal, epic quest for it, in Dignan's and in Anthony's, as Anthony puts it to Inez, "totally lost" lives (though one of the many differences between Dignan and Anthony is that Anthony knows he is an "unhappy person," whereas the former, ever quixotic, thinks things are going swimmingly, as his silly observation "crime does pay" attests). A far more important, symmetrical, aesthetically whole, and artistic film than has been, as it seems to me, heretofore acknowledged, *Bottle Rocket* is also profoundly exemplary of Godard's famous dictum that in order to make a film all you need is "a girl and a gun." But we'll get to that in a bit.

From the very outset of the picture Anderson's subtle whimsies—the little touches he's renowned for—are in full flower: Dignan, flamboyantly and boyishly garbed in ridiculous lawn tennis whites, "hiding" in the bushes outside Anthony's window, looks much like an inmate of (or janitor at, or minder in—one thinks of the draconican nuthouse "handlers" in Forman's classic *One Flew Over the Cuckoo's Nest*) the very asylum he's "springing" his friend from. He looks like he should be working at an ice cream truck like the one that appears later on and that Dignan buys cones from for Mr. Henry. Dignan's sui generis, a nutter, albeit a loveable one. He's the one who could've used more than a bit of Dr. Nichols' therapy ("You've been a great doctor," Anthony needlessly tells him, in that Anthony hasn't really needed psychological counseling; he's needed a job, some purpose in life). Though the fact that Dignan mistakes Dr. Nichols for "the janitor" that "smart" Anthony, Dignan imagines, has "bribed" suggests that he, Dignan, wouldn't recognize proper "help" if it hit him on the head with a lavishly framed psychiatrist's diploma.

Conspicuous to a comic fault, Dignan's hardly dressed for the initial operation / occasion (a motif that'll find a ludicrous parallel in the egregious orange jumpsuit he affects and kits his "crew" out in for the disastrous ultimate warehouse heist) in that, of course, all-white attire is the last thing you'd don when you are looking to camouflage yourself. Which is the last thing, anyway, that Dignan really wants to do, metaphorically speaking. Most post post-Freudian / modern psychologists maintain that recognition, not happiness, is what we crave and go after more than anything: not especially as in gold medals and blue ribbons, but more like "I see you for who you are, the real you." With a dose or dash or splash of blue and gold. Dignan's desperate quest for recognition finds an ironic trope in the heist mirror he should hold up to himself from an "insight" perspective, rather than flashing about, signaling unwitting distress. He should be trying to see rather than picture himself—as in the way he conceives of (or casts) himself as the "star" (cf. the bookstore heist meeting where D refers to Bob as "the zero," Anthony as the "X," and himself as the aforesaid metaphor) of an "operation" or caper— or a caper picture. But when we first meet him what we don't know, of course, is he hasn't suffered enough yet to warrant such self-knowledge, nor has he an inkling of being even close to aware of the fact that know(ing) thyself is something he should be striving for. In fact, facts (rather than revelations or epiphanies) are—as with most people who bury their consciousness in concerns with the outer rather than inner world—what Dignan concerns himself with, what he relies upon, much to his spiritual and emotional peril. As he tries to console / inspire his fellow "gang" member, Dignan, holding up the treasured picture of The Lawn Wranglers, lectures:

DIGNAN—*Fact: I learned more in the two months I spent with Mr. Henry than I did in fifteen years of academic study...*

ANTHONY, echoing his friend / "mentor" / "team leader," tells him—*Fact: Dignan, the picture's not doing it for me.*

Obviously oblivious to the not-funny pathos of his declaration, Dignan and Dignan alone is the palpable failure here. Yet, as the film bears out, he's no dummy, Dignan: he may have had only a couple of years of college (do the math on the "fifteen years"—unless of course Dignan flunked a year or two), but I often marvel at how eloquent he can be, and his lexical distinctions ("Don't treat me like the *jealous* friend that's *envious* of you," he tells Anthony in the diner scene) reveal the notion that he knows the meanings of words better than some college grads or even grad students might.

In contrast to Dignan, his "visionary" friend St. Anthony wants answers, not pie-in-the-sky potentialities and sentimental/pseudo-inspirational photographs. Anthony objects to and momentarily despairs over a hard cold world, the facts of life, the real world, one that's made his sister, aptly named Grace, "get so cynical." Obviously stung by Grace's hilariously less-than-soothing soothsaying ("How can you be exhausted? You haven't worked a day in your life!"), and feeling the veracity of her insinuation that he's "a failure," Anthony—one of the greatest of Anderson's boy/men creations—has yet to realize the profundity of his observation in the fine scene at the playground that he's an "adult" who's not really an adult—as so many Young Americans are:

GRACE—*What's going to happen to you, Anthony? When are you coming home?*

ANTHONY—*I can't come home, Grace…I'm an adult.*

He's not. Not yet, at least. He, too, hasn't suffered enough, hasn't yet fallen from grace, hasn't been humiliated to the point where true humility is acquired, earned; he's still too callow to assume full adult status and take control/charge of his out-of-control life, his future (an idea, as we'll examine, that's paralleled in the ingenious naming of Bob Mapplethorpe's hideously bullying brother, "Future Man"). Again unlike Dignan, who looks forward to going home, to the wrong home ("Till we say: 'Mr. H, we are coming home!'"), Anthony knows better.

Like many out-of-control souls, Dignan's a control freak, one whose bumptious charm masks his obligatory fear and mistrust of others. While Future Man "beats the shit" out of brother Bob "every day," Dignan hectors, belittles, commands, and otherwise browbeats his two untrusted "associates"—a thuggish euphemism Anthony picks up and employs, even in his conversation with his solicitous little sister. We get the sense that there's a real symbiosis here, one that's characteristic of many close but questionable friendships. (It's no coincidence that Grace is deeply, demonstrably disappointed when she learns that Dignan is one of the "associates" her brother's picked up again, as it were, now that he's back from "the desert:" "Dignan?" she sighs. "Yes, Dignan. And some others…" "What? I thought you liked Dignan?" "I do like Dignan," Grace retorts, "but he's a liar." Here Anderson puts on show the maxim that "Out of the mouths of babes, etc.") In other words, it's apparent that Anthony lets Dignan lead him astray, up the garden path, on account of he's so fond of his irresistibly gung-ho, ostensibly less-fortunate friend: "Look how excited he is," Anthony tells Dr. Nichols who is understandably worried about how "This [Anthony climbing down a ladder of linked-up bedsheets] doesn't look good."

Bottle Rocket opens with a shot of a room in a sanatorium and closes at a prison and prison yard—semi-parallelism in that both sorts of edifices symbolize at once exile and community, albeit marginalized ones, with their own formidable and perhaps comparable sets of rules and regulations. "We both respond to structure," D tells A, on the Greyhound Bus from Arizona back to Texas. But the prison house has too much structure/stricture, and the nuthouse doesn't have enough. The prison house is Dignan's future home where, some might argue, *he actually wants if not yearns to be.* For "the joint" is where most "legit" crooks end up— especially in the movies—and it is where Dignan'll thrive and indeed receive a sort of ultimate, twisted kind of recognition. To paraphrase D. H. Lawrence: the man who is murdered somehow wants to be.

In Anthony's case, the nuthouse is not so much a place to learn about oneself, to heal, and to acquire a bit of discipline as it is an *escape*—from reality, from responsibility, from pretty much everything. Anthony therefore "escapes" from a place of "escape." *Mise en abyme*. No wonder Dignan, post "going on the lam," feeling sorry for himself, laid out on the grass in the middle of nowhere once the hot-wired convertible craps out, laments: "Did it ever occur to you that your old pal Dignan would've enjoyed a great stay at some mental hospital out in the middle of nowhere? Going running at night, getting a tan with a bunch of beautiful girls? Did you ever think about that? What do you think Dignan was doing the whole time you were out there, man? I told you Dignan got fired, out on his ass. But you never thought about that, did you?" The speech is at once deeply manipulative and affectingly heartfelt, a signpost of Dignan's simple complexity. And the fact that it's couched in third person bespeaks Dignan's essential disembodied/ disenfranchised self here—as well as supplementing the telling/making up one's own story's theme of self-reflexivity. He's even lying on his back while he narrates it; and tells it to himself, as a sort of palliative, as much as to Anthony Adams. Stories mollify. And story*telling* mollifies, as Anderson seems to want to remind us here.

As we explicate the opening of the film, we'll see how it sets the tone for the life story ("And so it begins!" Dignan declares on the bus) that Dignan and Anthony (and by extension Anderson) are self-referentially "writing." The first sound we hear, after the title shot, is of something being richly *sparked*. But sparks often lead to and are harbingers of things blowing up (not always in a good way). Next we clock Anthony opening a window—a window, we might add, of reverse opportunity, for there's Dignan, hardly obscured by the bush he "hides" behind, signaling like a bumbling Tenderfoot Boy Scout, *caw-caw*ing down the lane in a cheap-o, useless, if not counterproductive, tone. How could anything, much less a mere shrub, hide someone so much larger-than-life, as it were, anyway? Dignan, like truth and murder in the old twin adages, *will out*. As the jaunty, fluted, trebly guitar-riffing, rim shot–laden opening instrumental by Mark Mothersbaugh rolls, *we* think (*with* Dr. Nichols as he spies an odd scene):

"What's this? What's going on?" That Anthony doesn't "have the heart to tell [Dignan] no" points up how his own compassion stands in both his and his friend's way: for a true friend would tell Dignan that to stage a breakout from a "voluntary hospital" is an act of indulgence at best, madness at worst. The "success" of the "break out" precipitates other capers. Had Anthony told Dignan, "Look, I can come home anytime I want; don't come here and bust me out of this place—you're wasting your time," then there wouldn't, most likely, have been a bookstore heist and a Cold Storage caper. The entire tale Dignan and Anthony (and Anderson) are telling mightn't have gotten "written" had A just said no.

Thus far, we've emphasized Dignan's likeable if not charming character, but Anthony's endearing as well, the kind of cool guy you just know you'd be friends with in real life, have a good time with. He knows just what to say to people, flattering Dr. Nichols when it's evident he, Anthony, has hardly needed real psychiatric help; and the fact that he waves goodbye to a number of people at the hospital suggests he's been liked, that he's been a kind, positive if not revered force (just like what he'll be after the first "going on the lam," "on the run from Johnny Law," runs its course and he gets his "life back on track" with two jobs and a coaching position for a junior soccer team).

"Any problems?" D inquires as A joins him. No. Of course not. Dignan will provide those. The melancholy wave and wistful look on Dr. Nichols' worried face should suffice to tell us, as he's observed earlier: "This doesn't look good." And things in general, of course, can't look good when one friend's fucked up on gangster movies and the other's too fond (in both senses—foolish, too) to resist him and his daft and excessively juvenile (delinquent) schemes.

"Driver, what's our ETA?" Dignan enquires as the Greyhound Bus rolls east into the sunrise. Digan just assumes an air or aura of importance here, ludicrously *autho*ritative, declaring absurdly, "We're on schedule." Then the real schedule—or Dignan's controlling plot or plan—emerges, and from a college-ruled school notebook, significantly. "A rough sketch of what *I* was trying to do," unveils not only Dignan's grandiloquent delusions and cluelessness to the fact that life can't be planned for (not "The Next Fifty," at least), but also his misguided efforts on Anthony's behalf—steps he has no business taking, plans he has no business making, despite the "impressive" fact that, in the sketchbook/college-ruled notebook, their lives are broken up into colorful (in both senses) chapters, just like a real book might be: "Wives and Family," "Living into 21st Century," etc.

On the bus home (though we know, as Anthony in the scene with Grace notes, you can never go home) Anthony jokes, while Dignan controls: "Did you enjoy your first visit to the nuthouse?" Anthony quips. Dignan responds firmly: "Be *sensitive* to the fact that other people are not comfortable talking about emotional disturbances…" Ironically, Dignan hardly is himself: sensitive, that is.

"And so it begins."

What begins is Anthony's and Dignan's story. A doomed one, a dead end—like all hyperderivative narratives. A road/story to nowhere, but one that has to be taken or told in order for it to be discarded, gotten over, so that one can go on, grow up, get on with it. Like jettisoned novelistic juvenalia, or a fledgling film a filmmaker hopes none of his or her following ever comes across, it pulls from the deepest part of the vault. It's a story made up for no real end or purpose, just because. An indulgent indulgence or daydream come to vivid life, writ large (or small). Certainly a story that "leads to Mr. Henry" can't end well—for, though we don't know it yet, Mr. Henry is the dark side, Dignan's evil twin/

father/double, the "sick, sadistic side" of Dignan we learn of (and perhaps don't believe in) after Bob has flown "the coop." Speaking of phrases like the above, we're made comically aware of the fact that Dignan often traffics in clichés, platitudes. "That's good cardiovascular," he opines as he learns that Anthony has been running ten miles a day out in the desert, getting in shape—a luxury the neurotic, image-conscious upper classes can readily afford. "Sit-ups, roadworks, hitting the bags"—these are words, not achievable goals. Dignan's sincerity is immediately called into question as Anthony notes that he's never known his friend to be "all that athletic." Dignan's defensive response reveals that Anthony has touched a nerve: "Does it sound weird—to be talking about all the exercise?"

As Love's frenetic, anthemic "7 and 7 Is" plays, we're, along with the two practiced burglars, thrust into action—the first burglary, of Anthony's house. Anderson's lauded/derided attention to detail/nostalgia/overt quirkiness comes to the fore, to memorable initial fruition here as Anthony takes time out from "robbing" to straighten some plastic or tin toy soldiers on his desk. Which "action" suggests two things: he likes things to be in their proper place; he's still at the age where he plays with things, fantasizes. *When I was a boy I thought about the times I'd be a man, / I'd sit inside a bottle and pretend I was in a can* Arthur Lee of Love wails; and the rollicking-classic sixties song is perfect for the jejune, naïf scenario.

In the aftermath, at the dime store or pharmacy lunch counter, D and A wax both nostalgic and "critical." "Not very thorough: left a lot of valuables behind," Dignan digs. "But that was one of the limitations of this job." What's also been left behind is some semblance of or being-in-touch with reality. Though not completely: in disgust Anthony walks away from the pinball machine upon learning that Dignan's taken Anthony's mother's earrings—something he wasn't supposed to do. Anthony knows Dignan's not to be trusted, though Anthony's most hopeful self frequently wishes Dignan himself would prove him wrong, prove him not to be so very relentlessly, well, Dignanish: Grace has told him as much—well before the playground scene, we imagine. And as he in a huff, pissed that he's been fooled again, exits the shop, Anthony mutters something *to himself* about how he knows better: "It's my fault. It's like, 'ultimately, Anthony, when you gonna learn?'" Learn that Dignan's world, his plans, and stories will lead to disappointment and betrayal. It is important to note here that Anthony, like a good friend, blames himself, not Dignan. Dignan, selfish and self-absorbed (however raffishly likeable) and recognizing all of zero limitations of the life/journey he's embarked on, is only concerned with more play, more control: "Man, you've got another ball!" he carps, admonishes, deflecting blame/responsibility, escaping into yet another game world. "Should I play your game?" he says to no one—a ridiculous notion, anyway. For the only games Dignan's playing (till all games stop and incarceration's an inescapable eventuality) are his own.

"Maybe we should've robbed your house—no, I bet that never crossed your mind," Anthony, out in the street as Dignan chases after him, goes in quest of him, remonstrates. Of course Dignan's compelled to run after his friend: how can he have a team, be a team leader, without a team, or at least one follower or disciple? How can he get back to where it all leads to, "to Mr. Henry," Dignan's anti-spiritual "father," without someone to take his lead, carry out his cockamamie schemes, listen to his stories, parallel stories to the stories Dignan's heard when he was part of Mr. Henry's "crew"? Dignan needs Anthony much more than

Anthony needs Dignan, though only the former realizes that thus far.

In the next scene, at Grace's elementary school (Catholic, looks like), Anderson's dizzy camerawork immediately *swirls* as a sort of mimetic gesture that evokes the "lost" person Anthony at this stage truly is. Then it "finds" Grace. This is thus first in a series of Andersonian tropes where grown-ups consult kids, come to them for advice (cf. Mr. Blume asking Max "What's the secret?" and Royal caucusing on the Y rooftop with Chas's boys re: what to do about their hostile-to-him father). "She is a *cute* little kid," Dignan observes, though he only sees the surface of people, even child-people, sometimes, not the fact that Grace is/has something more, something deeper than mere cuteness, that she is a real person with real worries and valid "criticisms" of things/people that might lead her brother astray, people like Dignan, in other words.

As Dignan and Bob and Anthony drive away from another scene of disappointment and ostensible failure ("How'd it go with Grace?" Dignan nosily inquires, ignoring Anthony's distraught deflection/response: "Can we please just go, Bob?"). It's a failure only A recognizes and, much to his chagrin, acknowledges. Later on, when he has his shit together, Anthony will write to his kid sister from Bob's house where he goes to live instead of going home or continuing "on the lam" with Dignan. In his letter he'll assume a much more fraternal if not avuncular tone, counseling Grace rather than being counseled by her. Although his advice ("Learn a foreign language") is somewhat comically solipsistic, given his communication troubles with Inez and significant things getting lost and embarrassingly revealed in translation ("I mean, last night when we had sex it was..."), Anthony's intentions are good if not pure. He doesn't want Grace to worry (she seems really worried at the playground, unduly and prematurely burdened); he doesn't want her to be able to say that he hasn't worked a day in his life; she *can't* say that now that he has two jobs and a coaching gig. He wants to make amends—for putting Grace in a compromised position (having to put the earrings back) and for chastising her for getting into "the habit of asking a *huge* amount of questions." He wants to atone for sounding like censorious Dignan, his "bad" friend.

"What has she [Grace] ever accomplished with her life that's so great?" Dignan, in the shot outside the car, bathetically kvetches. And we're meant to laugh. *At* not *with* him.

Many of us have had a "bad" friend. Most of us grow out of hanging around them/grow away from them. When we're ready to, that is. Anthony's obviously not ready. Nor will he ever be, really. He'll continue to watch out for/watch over Dignan till the very end, and till the very end of the picture. And just as Anthony conducts a so-to-speak reverse-role interview with Grace, so does Dignan, in the ensuing scene, quiz Bob Mapplethorpe about his "potential" as a getaway driver. The typical Andersonian deft, literaryish symmetry. Whereas Dignan is, as Grace avers, "a liar," Bob tells the truth: "I really wanna be a part of this team, and I'm the only one with a car." Why, we might ask here, is Bob the only one with a car? Possibilities: Dignan's been fired from Mr. Henry and he's broke—unlike Bob and Anthony, he doesn't come from money; Anthony hasn't earned a car—or he's had no need for one (sweet, accommodating sorority girl Elizabeth maybe was happy to drive, and "out in the desert" he hasn't needed one and the responsibilities that come with it, anyway).

Bob's *audition* (cf. movies/self-reflexive motif, plus the obvious/curious last name here that harks back to the notorious American photographer) succeeds; Dignan tells him, "That's good." Good as

in good for Dignan and his self-oriented purposes—
not good as in moral or ethical. But of course. And
Dignan is hit "right here," in the heart, in his most
insincerely sincere/actorish spot. With his greased-
back hair, his underworldish, *corroded* old Merc, and
his cheap, black, thrift shop sport coat, Bob's the
sort of sap or chump or rube who's perfect for the
"role" of sidekick and pawn. He *looks* like an actor:
a puffy, ignominious, two-bit bit-player extra from
a Godard or Truffaut picture—or someone who
wasn't scary-looking enough to make the cut for a
Scorsese joint. Dignan, Anthony, Bob, Future Man,
et alia are bored, alienated, unhappy, underachieving
suburban kids with little to look forward to and less
actually to do. What should they do? What *can* they
do? Finish college? Then what? Get a job? Then
what? Be what everybody else is: normal, average,
similar. Carve out a life you'd eventually like to
escape from—as Bob and Future Man's parents
have done. A life of mega-privilege is no life, really,
at all. For instance, Bob and Future Man belong to
a country club, one of the advantages of which, as
Bob amusingly explains, is "you can sign" for things
and not pay for them. You can forge your own
signature. This choice line puts us in mind of the
fact that if there's one thing us grown-ups know it's
that you must pay—there's no such thing as a free
lunch, not even at the club.

Apropos of the self-referential theme I'm attempting to trace, the practice heist, we should note, is a bookstore job. Ripping off a place where *stories* are *sold*. Hollywood much? Smartly, Anderson didn't have the boys rob a movie theater: that'd be too pat, in terms of self-reflexivity, and might prompt such wonderings as: "Isn't the director ripping off quote-unquote 'The Movies' enough not to have to hit us over the head with it? Isn't it enough that, in homage to past master Mike Nichols, Anderson has given Anthony's doctor that very name?" Stupidly, the boys choose an industry that generates way less revenue than the silver screen does; or maybe they (read: Dignan) reckon that pacific booksellers would offer less resistance than a wannabeish ticket taker who's seen *Mean Streets* or *Goodfellas* five nights straight and is itching for a brouhaha, for some "bona fide action." A bookstore job must be safer—a training wheels kinda thing.

Love—not the band, though they'll want discussing. There's no clearer evidence that Dignan is starved for love than in the poolside scene where we are introduced to Stacy Sinclair, the in-tow sorority sister who seems to be friends with brutish Future Man and dull, thuggish Clay. As she kneels before St. Anthony, she hardly seems to see Dignan—from her position of adoration and in general. Why? First of all, because she's evidently too smitten by his cuter friend (one who's dated Elizabeth, who we are lead to imagine is both "hot" and rich—the kind of girl whose family has a beach house where you can "lay out at" and go waterskiing; plus there's that element/phenomenon where sorority girls often go in pursuit of guys their "sisters" have dated, especially if the gal-precursor was something of a cynosure or queen). Secondly because Dignan, in a way, isn't there: he's invisible, he doesn't exist. Not really. Perhaps on account of he's put no or very little effort into getting them, girls. (He's been too busy, he might plead, coming up with fifty-year plans, thinking about "our" future, and lucklessly apprenticing himself to Mr. Henry.) Though it's clear he wants recognition from females—or from a total babe like Stacy, for sure. "His name's Anthony and my name's Dignan," he states, but (and it must sting him, smart somewhat) she doesn't even look his way.

And no wonder Dignan has no game, gets no play, as it were: unlike normal young heterosexual men whose fundamental concerns are with, as Max in *Rushmore* puts it, "scoring chicks" ("That's all anybody seems to care about," he laments to his dad), the guys in *Bottle Rocket* play pinball, make and sign pacts ("I know you remember the list 'cause you signed it—'Things Dignan's not supposed to touch.'"), ride mini-bikes, tool around in yuppie trucks, jog, squabble, backstab ("How does an asshole like Bob get such a great kitchen?"), have little pouty spats with one another, rig up a pretend/practice heist, shoot handguns at makeshift/rogue ranges (making faces like tough guys, brandishing pistols in cowboy style), take bus trips, have fistfights, grow "entire marijuana crop[s] in [my] parents' backyard," sit by the pool having Tom Collinses and white bread sandwiches, mangle language ("How much bullets does this thing take?" Bob wonders), shoot off fireworks, play make-believe (robbing Anthony's house), and eat kiddie food (burgers and milkshakes, French fries in bed for Dignan when he gets a split lip in a preposterous bar fight). They're grown children.

In one deleted scene, a tall fat glass of cold milk quivers, sits on the table between Bob and Anthony. Where are the parents of these endearing Peter Pans whose collective childhoods have outstayed their welcome, we may well inquire? Anderson's world is a fantasy realm—a world without adult supervision, a never-never land of bogus aspirations and chuckleheaded pipe dreams. Bob's obviously well-to-do mom and dad (the house is gargantuan, the pool expensive-looking) are in Singapore—working or playing just like their kids are, we never find out. Anthony and Grace's mum and dad never materialize, and Dignan comes from a broken and likely less-well-off home—something we deduce from his line: "You know there's nothing to steal from my mom and Craig."

We should note that not only are the principal characters' parents absent, but women in general seem not to figure in these boy/men's slackerish, lollygagging lives—not, at least, till Inez comes along and totally rocks Anthony's small, psychotically closed world. With her kindness and compassion, Inez in fact senses this, that dorky "Jerry"/Dignan needs a hug. As he blathers on about recommending the (dismal hideout) motel Inez works at to his friends (what friends? Anthony has got to be his only friend; Bob's fully just an "associate"), the "little girl from Paraguay" cuts him off with an spontaneous and empathic embrace. Were Dignan ready to realize the significance of her pity (the hug is a gesture that smacks of how sorry she feels for him, how sad it is that he doesn't have a girl like the girl his friend's about to lose), he might pause for a moment and consider how wrong, if not dunderheaded, his objectives have been, are. But he's not ready. He's still the guy who conceives of himself as a veteran of a war that's entirely inside his head: "Thank you for listening to our war stories," he tells Inez—again bombastically, ludicrously. The war Dignan is fighting is not unlike all of his patron saint Don Quixote's battles against giants/windmills: illusory and as comically pathetic. Stories galore, encore.

Poolside, lemony drinks and white bread sandwiches organized delightfully, Anthony-who-is-not-a-liar tells flirty Stacy the truth—which Dignan, unsuccessfully, we might add, tries to deflect, casting meaningfully disapproving looks and sighing melodramatically, knowing he's the one who's being cut out here. "I went nuts… Do you really want to know?" Anthony asks, rightfully questioning her sincerity, from experience with these sorts of disingenuous chicks. "I really do," says she:

ANTHONY—*One morning, over at Elizabeth's beach house she asked me if I'd rather go waterskiing or lay out. And I realized that not only did I not want to answer that question, but I never wanted to answer another* *water-sports question, or see any of these people again for the rest of my life. Three days later I was on my way out to the desert and that was that.*

The archetypal three days before Anthony's respite/retreat from the world ought to give us some indication of the hagiographic element in *Bottle Rocket*. Psychologically, this speech is germane on account of it reveals our saint's recoiling from/reviling of the silly superficiality of the modern world, with its concern with fun, recreation, and looks. (Why else do people "lay out" but to look tan, look "better"?) Anthony's rejection of Elizabeth and her Greek associates is a kind of moral judgment: these idle people pose superfluous, not meaningful, questions. There are much better questions to ask ourselves/each other. At least Dignan's working for a higher power: even though that higher power may just be his own megalomaniacal self—or himself in the form of Mr. Henry. Or the ideals that gangster/caper movies foment and showcase. At least Dignan cares, *is* thinking, leading a twisted version of the examined life, unlike attractive, sirenlike, sorority girls and their beachy, hedonistic proclivities and activities. The speech above is played for (minor) laughs, but it's deadly serious: Anthony is, as Stacy lauds, "a really complicated person." But in trying "not to be," he's that rare thing, a modern philosopher. *His* walks on water won't be coming with the assist of wooden slats with neoprene bindings on them. Anderson panders here (and, to his great credit, not cloyingly) to those of us GDIs who may have been privy to scenes from but never were a part of Greek collegiate "life": the longhaired, contemplative types like Anthony himself, who think there *must* be more than this to one's existence, even in one's terrible twenties, than looking forward to how "[Elizabeth] is going to be so jealous I saw you here." Very easily, Anderson suggests in directing the toothsome actress who plays Stacy, Anthony could have swooped down on the overtly eager girl in front of him and ported her off to Girlfriendland—or even, one imagines, just for the proverbial roll in the hay. But hey, he's been there, done that. And besides, that'd constitute an act of desertion and betrayal. For Dignan, who holds sway over Anthony's concerns, is right there, right beside him, in a deck chair, not wrangling, not having to, unwittingly cockblocking, despite the fact that he, as he fancies himself a good friend, would never see or admit that in a million years. Stacy isn't part of Dignan's story/plan. She and her ilk aren't even footnotes, in pencil, penciled in.

Future Man. Let's consider him. Philosophically and as a caricature/character.

Future Man's the avatar of such ghastly orientations as social groups like frats and sorority's manifest, and his bullying of his brother is a more ticklish issue, though he's certainly got—via his association with Stacy—to be reckoned with as a shallow ally of the Elizabeths of this world. As Bob doesn't even remotely resemble Future Man, we might wonder "Is Bob adopted? A stepbrother and pariah?" Prudently enough, Anderson doesn't essay to explain the wickedness here (how can you account for relentless, inveterate malice anyway? Is Future Man *evil*—and what *is* evil? Does anyone really know? It's as fundamentally inexplicable/indefinable as love is, no?); but in turn we might wonder why Anthony and Dignan don't spring to Bob's side, aid him before Future Man "beats the crap" out of Bob once more, as any "good," loyal "gang member" might. Is that another gag on the director's part? Is there no stopping Future Man, just as there'd be no stopping the future? Anderson makes Andrew Wilson look pretty intimidating here, arms aggressively akimbo (Clay, too), looking around for someone to take his own frustrations out on, like a lumberjack off his meds, and Dignan visibly starts with fright as F swaggers up. Well, the answer to the question—why not try and stop the real bad guy that Future Man is?—is perhaps that this is no ordinary "gang" capable of action, of revenge or at least "getting" one of the guys who's "getting" one of their own. It's a rich kids' gang—and therefore "no gang," as Dignan, in frustration with Bob who plays with the flash (overlarge, overkill) silver gun, declares later. Or: only a superantihero like vicious, Jaguar-driving Mr. Henry is a match for such a one as the F-Man, so why try? Though the dialog is funny ("You're calling me a bully? I'll show you a bully!" Future Man yelps before he strikes), the serious situation it garnishes is hardly humorous. Bob is in real pain: and again. He's not been exaggerating à la Dignan when he tells his chums that he gets a beating "all the time." And for a mere leaf left in the pool. "It's a leaf," Dignan banally observes, proffering as little actual help as when he tells Bob that his brother "needs to hire an attorney" when he, Future Man, gets caught with the "entire" backyard marijuana crop. Bob's precipitate "opening up" in the car just after the Grace scene bears out that he's despairing, that he means it, that he's being real and that he's sincere. Why else would he join a "gang"? Bob doesn't like Dignan (who could or would?—only Anthony, and us, the viewers, who are at a safe cinematic vicarious distance from him), and Dignan doesn't like or respect Bob. They're just using one another—Dignan, Bob for Bob's car; Bob, Dignan for something "to be a part of." Bob acknowledges that he's "just not very good at this 'selling yourself' stuff;" that's *all* Dignan's good at—selling. A "picture" of a possible future, or the souls, in a manner of speaking, of his friends. To quasi-demonic Mr. Henry, eventually, "hopefully." If the laughs stopped coming in this subtly funny film, we think, we might let ourselves get really super bummed for these walking unholy trinities and pain merchants. "If you're feeling alone," Bob whinges, "like nobody in the world cares, like nobody fucking gives a shit, then I'm here. I'm ready to listen, man." Future Man sounds like the psycho and psychodramatic side of Dignan when he says, "What the fuck is this [leaf]? Bob, you were told to thoroughly clean the pool this morning."

Cut to the rifle range. Well, not an actual rifle range but a bucolic, impromptu, Rube Goldberged-up shooting-place near a north Texas ranch or farm house, a perfect locale to highlight how fundamentally impotent these characters are—as all gun-toting tough guys / cowboys are. The targets, drawn in childish scrawl, travesty true creativity; the poses posed are pathos personified. Though they don't know it, D and the gang and their activities are just as factitious as any frat's; what *fun* to shoot off a gun. One's put in mind here of the great line in Sam Mendes' *American Beauty* where Real Estate King Buddy tells Carolyn, his illicit and joyless paramour, in a remarkably velvety, plummy voice what *he* does whenever he's "stressed out:" *"I fire a gun."* Dignan, in this scene and predictably, picks the biggest and baddest-looking firearm: go large or go home. Though Bob, we'll find out, pays for it, pays the ineluctable price. Consider for a moment the notion of Chekhov's gun—how if there is a gun on stage, it's got to go off. And it will, wounding poor hapless harmless Applejack.

Other people pay for Dignan's "leadership" and masterminding—not Dignan himself. And Bob, in the following "meeting" scene where the bookstore heist is being plotted, and where, outside the cozy-comfortable house, romantic rain rains down, doesn't even get to play with the gun he paid for. "I paid for it!" Bob says. "Say that one more time," Dignan challenges his "associate" (a mafia term), again baiting him or any mother's son who stands in his way, waiting for it all to fall apart on account of Dignan deep down knows that somehow he's going to have to play the victim, end up one, be let down, suffer the fate all crime bosses suffer, end where all honchos and hidalgos end—from Macbeth on down to your latest cinematic Don Somebody or Godfather, *capo di tutti capi*. "Are the explosives really necessary here?" Anthony, who, true to his word, is "trying to keep it simple here." Which Dignan, unimaginatively, hampered by his idée fixe, takes as something "undermining." "I can't focus unless the gun is on the table," Dignan crazily asseverates, his obsessive-compulsive nature, intermittently repressed, emerging once more. "I paid for it!" Bob states. *Fact*. But Dignan only likes facts *he* marshals to support his theories and beliefs and hopes and dreams. And Anthony, wrangling kindly, peacemaking, brings D back from the kitchen where he childishly pouts and petulantly laments. So that Bob can listen—listen to Dignan's issues, to his own picayune, emotionally improvident despair over whether "we" are a "team" or not. "Hey," Anthony consoles, reassures, his eyes glossy with fraternal concern if not love for his friend, "we are a team." Bob's not so sold, however. In one of the funniest/quirkiest lines in the film he nods unconvincingly and goes: "Yeah…team." In the smallest, most halting voice imaginable. Classic Anderson. And "harmony" and "unity" are restored—if but for a moment. For hard upon it comes Dignan's classically insensitive *casting* of Bob as "the *zero* out here in the car." Brilliant. Of course Dignan's "the star;" Anthony, an x-factor, is "the x;" and Bob, who is nothing to Dignan but an associate—expendable, superfluous—is…nothing.

An "at-night" shot, shot through with an ominously muffled heartbeat soundtrack for pumped-up/jumped-up adrenaline's sake. The zany tape on the broken nose and on the not-broken one. The boys in costume, Hamletish, customary black for maximum capering. "Exactly!" The Freudian "let's get lucky!" urging from Dignan as he and Anthony, at long last, spring into criminal action. "*Caw-caws*" encore. Bob doing a mouth-bird-hand sound by way of absurd "answer." (It's an owl sound—the mythopoeic bird of omens, albeit, in this case, unheeded ones.) This scene could be one of tyro-artist Max Fischer's plays—it's a rip-off and *a rip-off.* "Stretch," the book clerk Anderson'll cast again in the opening scene of *Rushmore* (to our great delight: the underused Dipak Pallana), goes with the flow here, almost like an accomplice himself. How could these heistmeisters be resisted? Look how excited they are. Too excited. For manners fall by the wayside in the wake of their excitement.

Dignan, who is often remarkably polite (as all suburban American boys, irrespective of their class status, are taught to be), forgets himself and calls the manager an "idiot." Until he's called out on it, his rudeness: "Don't call me an idiot," the manager guy hisses. And D backs off, maybe having a minor realization that crude and rude is no way to go in facilitating a robbery. "Do you have bigger bags, for atlases or dictionaries?" Dignan, reversing field, backing way the fuck off, asks nicely; anybody but him would be disembarrassed here of the notion that they're cut out for a life of crime. "Sir…" Dignan ads decorously, respectfully. It's such a great touch/scene. "Quickly…do your best," Dignan, doing his worst, urges. "I want everybody…just sit tight, sit tight. Thank you so much."

With a deft, genteel, comic touch, Anderson has Anthony, as he tools down the aisles, pick up a random text from the "Government" section, ostensibly, one that chronicles "Jobs in Government 1995." With little self-governance in evidence here, there's little chance of that. "Success, full success," Dignan announces, before the getaway car has even gotten away. Before it's even started.

Back at Bob's, hard-bitten-guy whiskey bottle in hand, Digs does a dance of celebration, samba-ing with panache, jokes to Bob that "although his share won't be as big," he, Bob, "gets the Spirit Award." What the heck, Dignan? No James Cagney or Jean-Paul Belmondo ever gave one of his guys such a Boy Scoutish "award," not even in jest! What are you thinking? As Bob gets up to protest getting less dosh, Dignan backs off: "Did you see the look he gave me? Don't cross this guy. Don't even think it." The team leader wants his team to be tough like he is; he jibes and jives and goads magniloquently. But Anthony and Bob, having "pulled off" the smallest of small heists, are like the grunts in Kubrick's *Full Metal Jacket*—"the phony tough and the crazy brave." With emphasis on the latter adjective.

"So, Dignan, what's next?" Anthony, childlike, wonders, eager for his/their story to exfoliate further. His "boss" whoa-whoa's him, self-referentially: "Everybody [ha! all two of them; plus us, the viewers] wants to know what happens next! May I enjoy this moment?" But the moment's spoiled by the truth, by reality. The picture. The very picture of The Lawn Wranglers, a mere image (of an image, like a *mise en abyme*) betrays Dignan as Anthony, via a rather if not understandably-so smug Bob, learns the truth that "the crew" is but a landscaping/gardening team—not a big time crime syndicate, as D would grandiosely have "everyone" think. "What do you mean, landscaping?" Anthony asks—as though it were some sort of code he's not been apprised of as yet. "Push the mower, trim the hedge," Bob scoffs, pfffts. Score one for poor, cut-rate "cut-throat" Bob who's ever ready to wax paranoid about being "cut out." He doesn't trust Dignan. He's never trusted Dignan. And well he shouldn't. Cue shit-eating grins all-round, facing *facts* rather than reductively stating them. How's good/bad old Dignan gonna talk his way out of this one? Cut to the boys on the lam, gassing up Bob's thirsty Merc, expensive, conspicuous, and not easy to fix, the *last* getaway car (save a VW van) you'd ever favor, not in rural Texas, certainly. "Yes, yes they're landscapers," Dignan admits, "but did it ever occur to you that a landscaper's a perfect front for an operation, man?" One truth leads to another, scaffolds it: for here we along with A learn that D's been fired. By a "very talented thief." (A harbinger of a later, bigger, inevitable, and very classic cinema-esque betrayal perp'd by Mr. Henry at the end of the film as he cleans out Bob's house while the boys pull the outrageously ill-conceived and even more ill-executed warehouse scam.) The Lawn Wranglers has been "the best job I ever had," Dignan testifies. Well, it's been a real job, at least, a job job, not a heist job. One of the great things about it, his job with Mr. Henry, has been that it's afforded Dignan the opportunity to listen to *stories*. Bad guy yarns, presumably.

"Listening to stories…" Dignan says self-reflexively, waxing nostalgic for something poetic in his less-than-epic life. Calamities come, Anderson hints, when fuck-ups and emotional illiterates take pen in hand and try and write their own. Anderson's intimated in interviews that he likes to watch characters come unglued, that he finds humor in that in particular. Dignan, and Dignan's "story," is unraveling fast—and he's scrambling to stitch or superglue or what-have-you it back together for both himself and "for" Anthony, upon whom he seems to codependently depend. The story of Dignan's sacking embodies real, palpable Dignan-pain as well: "'Dignan—you're out.'" Mr. Henry callously tells him: "Just like that." The swift, unmerciful hand of injustice is something Dignan's felt on his ass, and it's scarred him, given him a chip on his shoulder *and* a cross to bear there. Dignan grows a bit here, just a smidge, he credits Mr. H. for being right about firing him: "Just because it's a front doesn't mean someone doesn't have to do the actual landscaping." Great writing and filming and colorful character development. "But those days are over now," Dignan goes on, enrolling himself mentally in beginning intermediate sagacity. Yet he's not "there" yet, at a place where he can "see" himself or others clearly; for ill-advisedly, as I have noted, D looks forward still to getting involved with, mixed up with, the nefarious Abe. "So don't worry about your future 'cause *I am thinking,*" Cartesian D tells Augustinian A. And that's, as we now must realize, exactly what A should do: worry. Donning sunglasses that look more appropriate for a jaunt to Elizabeth's parents' beach house than for an underworld baron, Dignan spouts a memorable, much-loved, modified, paraphrased, made-up or Dignanized line cribbed from a putative caper picture: "On the run from Johnny Law— it ain't no trip to Cleveland." Or is that an actual quotation from some super obscure "B" movie, a line Anderson misremembered somehow or cribbed? Does it matter—when it's all made up in Dignan's narratal head—anyway? *May* he just enjoy this moment, this moment with himself, self-satisfied and marveling at his own "powers"? It's an almost-soliloquy, this scene, writ not large but fittingly little. It isn't Hamlet, or Roland, nor is it Romeo, nor taciturn Heathcliff. But it's key, a kind of stupid genius.

And we jump to a fireworks stand, again near open fields and fallow farmland, in the middle of Nowhere, Texas, so the boys can spend some of their "shares" on boy's toys, the eponymous bottle rockets, fireworks *sans* firearms. "Zorro is Back," the jaunty-happy song by Oliver Onions that merrily-liltingly plays, is rife with ripe irony. *"Used to being free...la la la la,"* it goes. Free? Yeah, sure. Tell me about it. The road, being on the lam, on the run from Johnny Law—these are mere illusions of freedom, perilous parodies of such. Here, there, and everywhere, wherever you go, there *you* are—and Dignan, he's there as well, sure as shit, as death and taxes. This flavor of freedom's just another word for a trap, one A and D and B don't see. Not yet. Well, until night falls and saintly Anthony, realist, guardian angel, begins to perceive in the strange-town darkness how things really stand. He doesn't think Dignan's "happiness" is "appropriate." He sounds like his censorious, monitoring friend. But it's dawning on him that the gang's going nowhere fast, *is* nowhere. "Your seventy-five year plan does not seem to be working," he remonstrates. *Fact.* "The only thing I've learned is that crime does not pay." Forced to tone it down, Dignan grows coachlike, crypto-paternal, prototypically platitudinous: "That's not the greatest attitude in the world," he retorts lamely. Yet, of course, it's the right attitude to take—crime doesn't pay. Read for the portmanteau pun on "pay." Though irrepressible, unsinkable Dignan can't repress himself, the real (for now) him, for more than a minute; he tries to pacify his associates by telling them absurdly that he's going to get "the best room in the house," a house that's not a home, that can't even have one good room, on account of it's a motel, "a place to lie low"— it's literally a no-name no-tell, this establishment. The sign out front just reads "Motel." How much less glamorama can you get? The lying low cliché is ironic as well—in that the gang's already *laid low*, lying low, though not as low as they, as we'll find out in tandem with them, can go.

We've seen the gun; now where's the girl? Just as the boys are the embodiment of the American Scam, so is Inez a living doll (not in a pejorative sense, but because she's hardly a tough's "moll") that reps the American Dream. Her name's a Spanish or Portuguese variation of Agnes, meaning "pure or holy." She's *perfecto* for a saint like Anthony—she's one as well. "She's a serious person," Rocky (check *that* cinephile handle) counters, translating as A urges her to "come with us" after they've canoodled in a pool during a midnight swim and had great sex just once and partied and watched the Southwest sun set (plus lone ranging Dignan in a field) from a less-than-romantic balcony. "Tell Anthony I love him," Rocky tells "Jerry" at Inez's behest as the "gang," now missing one key, car-owning member, decides it has to mosey. How can she love him? She's "known" him two, maybe three days; he's never worked a day in his life, while she's good at and diligent about having one of the toughest US jobs: being a housekeeper, a housemaid(en). He'll idealize her, drawing her on horseback, like a heroine from an illustrated story, free and proud and individual, mythopoeic, "little *sparks* flying off her," as Anthony annotates. Sure as he's a guy in a uniform of sorts, the kind all girls go for (the uniform a parody of one, actually, a warm-up track star jacket and a Lancelot or Galahad haircut, preppy chinos, and Adidas). Surely, she's never met anyone like him, and he ostensibly her. So how can she? Well, this is the movies, after all. Shit happens. Magic shit happens. Standing in the aforementioned field, holding hands, looking adorable, already like a couple, how can we not root for them? They look so cute together; they're—without knowing it— not going to succumb to *egoisme à deux* like so many power(less) couples do; they're not going to cut "Jerry" out; love's made them even better people.

"Why don't you just come with us? Why don't you just come to this bar with us?" Anthony implores. "I don't wanna go," Dignan sulks. But A and I don't let him do that for long, and they sally forth to the *barra* (so that Dignan can get his ass kicked real good, but never mind that just yet, though cf. *Rushmore* and Max getting his thumped by Buchan, and Royal getting his kicked by life itself in *Tenenbaums*).

The first morning (after) shot shows our bandits sleeping motel-rough, catawampus as all get-out, the Spanish radio alarm going off without their having set it—or did Dignan, with an agenda for a plotless, aimless day? Anthony, up early, is already out at the pool, working out, perhaps, or used to getting up early as he must've done at the nuthouse. Emerging from reinvigorating water, the first thing he sees (in a most beautiful, hypercolorful shot) is no less than a vision of a beautiful girl, Inez herself, leggy-petite and slaving away, doing her difficult, melancholy job, looking lonely, looking diffidently ready for some excitement. The song that plays as the camera closes in on Anthony in order to suggest how smitten he is goes *"Que mala!"*—not to suggest something bad is about to happen but that Anthony's about to "have it bad" for someone. And it's about time we got some "scenery" happening here: a female presence is on the verge of long overdue. Of course, she's heartbreakingly barefoot (what *is* it about girls unshod?); he can't take his eyes off her, his look is one of respectful admiration, not ogling or lust, really. He's a Narcissus who survived. Inez ties her hair back and turns and catches him looking. He waves. She's not going to wave back: she's a serious person, most likely Hispanic-*Catolico*/Old World Traditional, and mindful of the fact that she works there, at the fleabag, and flirting's not allowed. When, later, in the room, Anthony introduces himself and they shake hands, she looks around first, hoping she won't get in trouble. Little does she know how much trouble she's already in. Which isn't much. It's only love.

The next shot shows Anthony with his hands dreamily stitched behind his head, refusing Dignan's request to get his haircut in order to "hide our identities." There's a girl in the *picture* now; A can't risk getting a bad haircut at a Podunk barbershop. No way. "Then you're going to have to dye it red 'cause we have to hide our identities," Dignan, bumbling once more, shouts. As off Dignan and Bob go to get haircuts, Anthony takes a reverse-romantic walk with "his" girl. The language barrier's not the only one, we'll find. He compliments her posture. Words sometimes get in the way. She knows what he means. Girls can tell. Her posture? She's a stand-up person, that's for certain. He is, too. But more of a dormant or nascent one. He makes a typical gringo mistake, assuming she's Mexican. She's already teaching him, making him better, schooling him to wait and not follow her into the rooms, advice he ignores, on account of he can't help himself.

"Paraguay," she says, lilting it with her beautiful little half-lisp. And he struggles to place it in his mind—though "lost" people aren't normally good with inner or outer geography. In an act that smacks of intimacy he holds a warm towel up to her cheek. How weird he must seem, tailing her as she goes about her a.m. tasks, assisting her (to the apparent surprise of a couple of checking-out guests) in his tatty bathrobe. (Anthony packed a *bathrobe* for going "on the lam"?)

Goddam Dignan can't help it either; at the barber's he's even talking to a customer, intimating that the haircut the guy's getting is one "my friend needs to get." Where the devil did Dignan get that shirt that's part Boys Pajamas Department and part LeisureWorld? Hardly helping Dignan hide his own unhideable identity. As Bob relays the bad news re:

crop and brother, Dignan's incredulous, getting caught—whether it's him or a rival—doesn't even enter his (un)consciousness! "They got him by the balls," D tough-talks. "What's the official charge?" he officiously-lamely inquires. Bob's incredulous as well. At Dignan. "You and I both know [Future Man's] not a drug dealer," Dignan self-centeredly says. As if that's enough, as if that suffices. But F's in a real jam, not a make-believe movie one. Something's got to be done—not just scribbled out in a notebook. "What about hiding our identities?" Dignan yodels in one of the film's funnier lines. Has there ever been a more inept bad guy in cinema than our D? He's an Inspector Clouseau alter-ego, him.

Back at the not-ranch, Inez and Anthony court and spark. She's got a locket—like some Medieval or Renaissance heroine. A wee picture of her sister who looks just like her. Anthony, bizarrely, asks to keep it as a keepsake or love-talisman. Later he'll give her a present in turn, his watch. Watches symbolizing, kinda, one's identity. *Your* watch and all of that. We reckon they're practically "going steady" now. "A little girl in Paraguay," Anthony rhapsodizes; he's making up stories about her now. *Their* narrative's begun. Importantly. The way he looks at her—what maid could resist *that?* The way she looks at him—who *is* this guy? A kind of romance-symbiosis.

Returning, Dignan thinks he's walked into the wrong room, as, in Bob's words, a "soiree" is going forward in there. "I guess there's been a mistake made," he says in the passive voice. But he's not talking about *the* significant mistake, of course— of embarking on a life of crime. The concerned and puzzled looks on the faces of the Latinos speak volumes: these *gueros* are not good news; that's something that's written all over their faces, "Jerry" and "Cornelius." Then, as the extended gang might've expected, Bob freaks out: *"Tengo un situation on* [sic] *mi familia!"* In the spat/discussion that follows it's apparent that D has taught B well: "You are pushing your luck, man!" Bob warns as Dignan dumbly advises that Future Man "needs to hire an attorney." A loyal bro, despite every reason not to be, Bob's already out of there. Before he even, next morning, early, "stole his car." For the moment, Anthony's wrangled Bob and set up a kind of truce. He's sincerely concerned for his friend Bob, yet as the next cut (the gorgeously shot and super-romantic bluey swimming-pool-blue pool scene) reveals, Inez has got to be right there, in his mind, an equal if not greater concern now. A girl like her doesn't come along every day, at every hideout spot, changing one's sheets, changing one's life. *"Que rico,"* as Inez says, indeed. Gentlemanly Anthony asks if he can kiss her (he's concerned, we imagine, with and about different cultures now; maybe Paraguayan girls, unlike most Yankee ladies, don't like a guy just to "make a move," and so it begins. Again. And along comes Dignan, cockblocking again. "Marco!" he burbles, like an impish ten-year-old. Kids about taking a dip. Sits down, declaring he's kidding and not that insensitive. Ha! Get out of here, "Jerry." You nerd with a classic nerd fake name. "No Lifeguard on Duty!" Dignan goons. He's the one who wants saving, natch.

And parting is such sweet sorrow. Not just for Anthony and Inez. But ironically and unsweetly, too, as Bob, with "no character," has flown the coop next morning. "We'll get him," Dignan announces, modifying some Jacobean revenge tragedy speech. Kinda. "And when we do get him, we'll blow up his car or something like that." And here comes the bit about the "sick, sadistic side" of Dignan, thinking about cruelly reveling in taking the look off "Bob's fat face." It's, to Dignan, an unforgiveable betrayal on Bob's part, though Anthony knows better and

that blood is thicker than etc. And another to follow
as D finds that A's known about Bob's (future) plans
to go back. Unbelievable.

A bit of comic relief's in order, Anderson
must've sensed, so we get the Denny's scene and
Dignan's professed happiness for his lucky friend.
Then a chaste lovemaking bit between the lovebirds,
with Love's "Alone Again Or" as the brilliant mood
music. *I could be in love with almost everyone*, Arthur
Lee sings. Which is the lovely effect Love and love
has on one.

Then "The Lonely Bull"–sounding trumpet
bit from Love and paradigmatic bottle rocket
loneliness (D fires one, significantly impotently,
into the ground) and the Dignan-gets-his-ass-kicked
scene. Naively, and thinking the best of his friend
still, Anthony can't believe the guy just decided to
jump D like that. Surely there was more to it than
that, given Dignan's penchant for asking for trouble.

Time to go, though. Dignan insists on "getting
the fuck out of this town." He's right. Though
Anthony's not gonna acquiesce to involving Inez
in helping them steal a car via nicking keys from
open rooms. He's taken enough, Dignan has—as
in "this is all I'm gonna take." Dignan grandstands:

"And this idea I don't back down from"—hot-wiring a car. Anthony has Inez, what does Dignan get? Anyway, *Amor Vincit Omnia*, hopeful Anthony must be hoping. Dignan "gives" Inez one more gift— the money. In having Dignan cluelessly hand over the obvious money-envelope to Inez, Anderson's in a fashion showing us how Dignan's his own accomplice in his own downfall(s).

"Who fears to rise will hardly get a fall," Anthony Trollope tells us in *The Eustace Diamonds*. Indeed.

But before the dynamic duo absconds, Anthony's gotta relay his epiphany about his love for Inez, a speech that involves metaphors of fog and lightning, allusions to being "totally lost" and now presumably "found" via Inez herself, love itself. An at once touching and ridiculous scenario, one that doesn't come across, on so many levels, in translation. And of course prudent and flattered Inez "can't go." Rightfully, she turns down Anthony's invite to Nowheresville. "Where are you going?" she asks meaningfully, ambiguously without knowing so. "She didn't love you, man," Dignan declares (wrongly?) when he learns Anthony has betrayed him further by giving "the housekeeper a five-hundred-dollar tip." "That's inexcusable," he states. Anthony's "story" of his and Inez's love—that hasn't worked, anyway. It's just a story. It sounds nice, but it's just that—something nice-sounding. Inez is more like Anthony than either realizes just yet. She wants practicalities, too. It's just that, well, Anthony's been hanging around with *someone* too long, too much. *"No es niguna razon. No tienes un 'plan.'"* The real world requires a real plan, a goal. "You're like trash," Rocky loosely translates. "Like paper—floating here and there...it doesn't sound so bad in Spanish." But the truth's gotta hurt A here. Must be cause for pause. *Fact.*

One more fight, a slap in the face, with a *wrench*, no less, and we're, for the moment, out—so that the inevitable can happen and the old friends can have a falling-out that'll set up a reconciliation and eventual redemption for both.

Back home, Anthony is back on track—work is redemption here, in this post-Protestant work ethic environment, gainful employment is king and the devil won't find "jobs" for not-idle hands. "We need to go home," A has declared as the convertible breaks down. Like the friendship's broken down. Anthony can't go home, not really, so he goes to Bob's home. Friendship again, Bob taking him in, working as a real team, in huffing-and-puffing tow as the more athletic chum takes him jogging, sporting a new track suit, signaling a real change, as they do things that are good for them, good cardiovascular—for their *hearts*, if you want to get mushy about it. The voiceover/letter to Grace admonishes her "to keep extremely busy—it's working for me." This is as sage as any homily by Dr. Johnson, who said basically the same thing about staving off loneliness. Anthony's got "a whole new program," it's the flip side of Dignan's program. A and B get up early, work, exercise, and are happy in getting it together, they "feel much better about" themselves. Though the dark side and Dignan are never far from Anthony's mind, as evidenced in Anthony's note that the soccer kids remind him of Dignan in that they're "no quitters." Despite the irony that Dignan should quit—quit dreaming and scheming dreamy schemes.

Out of sight but not out of mind, here comes Dignan in a threatening orange (a quasi-cautionary and *ugly* color, if you ask me) hot rod with Applejack driving. Uh-oh. He's apparently made his way back to Mr. Henry without anyone's help or manipulating involvement.

"Hey, Anthony—it's Dignan," the reconciliation scene begins. As if it could be anyone else. In his orange jumpsuit (he's already dressed for a prison stay) work clothes, Dignan trots up and it's understandably awkward: they've been so close, through so much, disappointed each other, blah, blah, blah. But true friendship, in Anderson's world, conquers all. Pleasantries, platitudes, apologies. Halting ones on Dignan's part—still the passive voice: "I wish that some of the stuff that was said out there…hadn't happened…by me." Endearing, charming, heartfelt, human, and therefore insufficient, really, but who's counting. A handshake. "Truce!" Dirk Calloway will proffer Max in *Rushmore*—an important Andersonian motif.

The dramatic catalyst for Anthony ill-advisedly going "back in" with Dignan comes, pointedly enough and not coincidentally, hard upon yet another shit-encounter with horrible Future Man. Given the choice between worlds where the Future Men of this world get to deride the Dignans (and call them "little bananas") and laugh at them for doing a job, Anthony makes the "right" choice—with stipulations, three "conditions," like three anti-fairy tale wishes. One of which—"Bob's on the team"—Dignan ain't gonna like. Dignan's mini-bike breaking down (another omen, another machine crapping out) ought to have been a warning for Anthony, but he's too loyal and good to see it; and besides, "Look how excited he is." And besides, poor guy, he's just been totally faced by cruel Future Man and Clay. "Did you see what he had on?" "Yeah, it was pretty cool." Same old blundering dunderhead, a not faux but real naïf. Anthony's "Goddammit!" has got to tell us he's doing this, getting involved again, against his better judgment.

Abe Henry. Mr. Henry. Who baptizes Dignan, his "son," with water, from a rooftop, where overgrown boys play and horseplay and carry-ons are carried out. He's a fucking dick, is what he is, unabashed. A "strongman" but not John Henry strong, an Abe but not an honest one. "It's locked!" Dignan says; is he worried about being locked out again? "No, no, no—come on, son," Mr. H, a trickster with a shark's tooth necklace, assures him. Then the water trick. "He poured more water on me," Dignan, a sap and lackey once more, aw-shucks. Real funny. Like the gag-introduction to Anthony. Real funny. A real fun guy. James Caan has never been more, well, James Caan. One of the last greats and ideal for the role of the real villain. In welcoming the boys to his HQ, he benedictorily touches D on the head. Old Abe's heart-to-heart and tête-à-tête with Anthony outside the ice cream truck is classic bad guy manipulative behavior, as Mr. H appeals to A's soft side and tells him he's "breaking [D's] heart." We note that Dignan here wears a turtleneck just like his "suave" hero. Guilting Anthony, Mr. H explains that Dignan "thought he had a team—turns out to be a man alone." You've let him down; you've gotta make it up to him; you owe it to him, is the "logic" here.

"Sick, sadistic" Mr. Henry spars, karate-style, with his *"producer,"* Rowboat. Producer? Seriously? Is Mr. Henry thinking of starting a film production studio as a new front, or is it just that he, like all big shots, talks tough, talks big, like when a singer in a rock band introduces you to "his" drummer. An odd but relevant term from Anderson, producer of self-referentialites. "Got the eye...got the other eye..." Abe triumphs. But they're just playacting, a choreographed fight, with Mr. H designedly meant to win, feed his "exotic" ego. He is someone to be leery/wary of. Like his "son." In the mini-bike scene, there's a shot of Bob peering from his bedroom window—afraid, we gather. And Anthony recoils a bit as Digs comes roaring up. Feeling his oats, Dignan's no force to fuck with again. But then the wrench of Future Man and his lackey (in cop-like sunglasses) and Anthony gets sucked back in while Bob, prudently, cowers.

At Bob's, in the second reconciliation scene, Dignan means business. Anthony has to do all he can to get them to make peace. "We are in the real world; we don't settle our problems with hugs," Dignan, ready to roll-up and square off, says—till Bob suckerpunches him, both suckers sucked back in. Tough talk—that ends in a hug.

Cut to the club and the lunch. The gang and Mr. H, swanning it swankily. Even kindly waiter Jackson's afraid of Future Man: "Uh-oh," he says and clears out. "Bob, fancy seeing you here...the rest of the gang," Future Man smarmily smirks. And knows not of what he speaks. Till Mr. Henry shows him who's boss—a fitting humiliation at the hands of a real bully. Adding insult to injury, he intimates to Bob that his brother's "a cocksucker." Beautifully cruel words from an ugly thug straight outta Dante or Dashiell Hammett. And a very literary and "noble" speech to go with them— Mr. Henry's quasi-Shakespearean moment:

MR. HENRY—*Johnathan. You know, Johnathan, the world needs dreamers. Though I don't think so. You know, John, one day, I believe, you're going to wake up and find you no longer have a brother, and you no longer have any friends; and on that day I'm going to be standing front and center just laughing my fucking head off. Hey, John!... John! Are we okay here?*

And a very brutal hand-wringing to go with those words of warning, that intimidating display of top-doggedness. Which we moviegoers watch with split interest: it's nice to see Future Man get a bit of comeuppance, but does it have to be at the hands of such a meanie as Abe? Pretty much. It's the way of the world. An odd and singular moment for a "comedy" flick. Andrew Wilson has stated that Caan wasn't fucking around in this scene: that his hand smarted and badly, wasn't fake-wrenched but genuinely mangled. Nice one. Nice. Bob's got a new hero: the gleeful look on his fat face is priceless. And the gang gangs-up on Jon with a hearty, callous laugh, spicing up the act of ridicule with a splash more derision. The team's coming together, and repairs to Bob's house. Big mistake. Mr. Henry honky tonks at the piano, wags his ass in everyone's face, entertains with a made-up song about how "Bob's gotta beautiful house"—one he'll "take care of" later by burgling, the betrayer betrayed theme on full display.

Cut to the stake out for the next job. Hinckley Cold Storage. Wes Anderson, did you have the crew rob a cold storage place just so that you can have the cops say "freeze!" when Dignan gets deservedly nabbed? In his eminently self-congratulatory fashion, Dignan's counting his chickens, because they've done the "legwork and the research." Fatal/ fateful words. Words someone "in Production" would use with respect to getting ready to film a film. "Creative" Anthony "illustrates" the scene with a little mock *storyboard*, a little homemade flip-book, one of someone *vaulting* over a bar. As if to say Dignan's still a hurdle? Someone he'll have to get over before he can be his own man/saint and get back to Inez where he belongs. Here, in a ditch, like a character in a Beckett play or novel, Dignan in a coat and tie, all "business," shines as he lauds Inez for being "a good person." Deep down, so is Dignan. He's just "a mixed up kid," just like what he accuses Rocky of being for saying "he loved me." And now Anthony understands; Inez did love him.

Q. Why doesn't he bail and hightail it back to her, right then and there? A. He's a loyal guy. There's something he said he was gonna do, and he's going, against his better judgment, to do it. More fool he. Anthony makes contact with her, Inez, to see if it's true. It is. "I do," she says when he asks her if she loves him. Her English is *great*. She's been growing too. "You're fluent now, Inez."

Mr. Henry's a con man, one in a preposterous kimono and topknot, so he's going to con his "kid" and suggest he "goes in there with you"—even though he's got other plans, Bob-related plans, of a bigger heisty nature. The son yearns to become independent, to prove himself. More fool him. "You've got the guts of a damn lion," Henry flatters. Had Dignan stayed in school long enough to read Machiavelli he'd know that the lion, the fox, and the wolf are buzz words and ominous ones. The party everyone attends rocks with sexy sax music. Not for long. Abrupt cut to the "job" site.

The capering caperers pulling (off)—or not—the final caper are, in their jumpsuits and with their new handles ("Bird Dog to Scarecrow"), a sight to behold—an at once homage to and send-up of innumerable heist job films, international and domestic. A tick-tock sounds throughout the early part of the scene—like a bomb ready to explode. Boyish walkie-talkies. Some are hardly boys, though. Kumar and Applejack are too old for this heist. Kumar's visibly out of it. "Let's get lucky," Dignan declaims again, but you don't get lucky twice in a heist. The repetition's a bad sign here. As is the fact that the getawaymobile is a VW bus—slowest of the slow and, again, conspicuous as all get-out. Manic mania and madness ensues. An utterly botched job. Kumar has lost his touch, and Dignan's never been in touch—with reality. Neither Bob nor Anthony really wants to do this job. Bob panics, predictably. Freaks again. There's a lot of running around, a team giving itself the run around. Does this bit ever remind me of the greatly inferior *The Life Aquatic*—a lot of running around to no purpose. "They've already seen our faces, Dignan!" "You are totally lost," Dignan declares to Kumar, echoing Anthony. Bob gets to fire his gun. Chekhov vindicated. "Did you ever have a touch to lose?" Dignan reels off, pissed, disappointed.

Sirens. The cops. "Who is in charge here?" Dignan pleas. "You are, you dumb son of a bitch," Anthony counters. Really? The inmates are running the etc. "You gotta give me this one!" Dignan, jonesing to be the star again, the hero, and go back in to the rescue, crows. "Dignan, you know what's gonna happen if you go back in there," A says. And of course Dignan, and we, has / have known all along what happens when you think crime does pay. Clearly, Dignan wants to be caught. How else is he going to get the ultimate recognition he's been questing after for so long now?

"They'll never catch me, man, 'cause I'm fucking innocent," says D in the film's greatest line. And he's right. And he's wrong. And to the darkly poppy tune of the Rolling Stones' forward-thinking "2000 Man" his destiny is met, his future's folded, sealed, "put on ice," the vast plans having met their poetic and predetermined end.

"Freeze!"

And this fine film might have ended there, with a self-referential freeze frame. But no, there's one more trinity to bear witness to, one more tribute to friendship and goodwill to make. As we cut from one yard, a work yard, to another, the prison, as Christmas music wafts through to show how time's passed, we see Bob and Anthony coming to "the joint" for a visit.

Just as Anthony's got a different tracksuit, Dignan's in a new jumpsuit, as white as his self-promulgated innocence, and he's humming a new tune, so to speak. He's not "out" like the friend he "sprung" at the film's beginning, but he's better, and he's better off. It's good that he's incarcerated. He's been in the prison of himself, his essential and existential self, for too long, all along, anyway. He belongs there, in the big house. Where he belongs. A two-year sentence. About enough time for him to finish his education.

A communion scene with burger and fries making an encore appearance brings us back in time to all the meals, happy and unhappy, the boys have shared. The scene could be a picnic lunch scene at a school, not prison, yard, complete with bleachers and exercise and socializing going on. Dignan has made something other than a mess: belt buckles. He's made more than just deranged plans, something tangible and practical. Growth's in effect here, in the house. "We did it, though, didn't we," Dignan vouchsafes—just like Anderson and his crew must've said after the arduous two-plus years it took to get this first film made; just like Anderson himself, taking a look, must've noticed that what he accomplished with this first and most seminal film was indeed, and perhaps to his aesthetic surprise, "in his own handwriting." Something he can recognize, something he will— years later (on account of the film flopped at first; "Criticisms…criticisms…")—get more than a modicum of recognition for.

Dignan's story's a sorry one, and one that's a muted triumph too. Dignan himself is sorry, truly so, that Mr. Henry's robbed Bob and that he, Dignan, is in part or even greatly to blame. Bob testifies: "In a strange way, it's brought me and Future Man closer together." And so does film itself, Anderson wants us to "get," bring us, through immemorial characters like these, closer together. We've been through something together. As a team. Way to go, team. "Uh-huh... team." Hi, Bob. Bye, Bob. "Just because you're a fuck up doesn't mean you're not my brother," Bob quotes Jon. The same could be said for the "brothers" archetypally three at the end of the film. Even Inez, part of the extended "family," is going to bring Dignan a *care* package. She cares. She should: Dignan, unbeknownst to him, has done much good in her life: he's brought her, gifted her with, albeit unintentionally, her true love and her saint...Anthony.

One last joke, one spoofy riff from the merry-melancholy prankster at the end, through the fence, as Dignan employs the old vernacular and "gotchas" the other two into thinking for a moment that they're back "in" again, in something that's now a *spring* job: "Did you bring that grappling hook? Are you ready? Bob, shield me from the bullets—they will *not* shoot at civilians." The pixie in Dignan's still there: the sly, wry look he gives shows us his (master) mind's still churning away—but not seriously now; that's all behind him; heists are things to joke about, probably because prison, being "in" in a different and very serious way, is no joking matter.

Isn't it funny that some things, and some people, never change—even though they themselves have transmogrified. And so "it" ends, *Bottle Rocket* itself ends with a self-reflexive self-referentiality: Anderson pointing up a narrative pointing up its own perfect, beauteous symmetry, "Isn't it funny how you used to be in the nuthouse and now I'm in jail?" Dignan notes, like an artist or director or savvy filmgoer or grad student in Film Studies might.

And, we may have vicariously learned, you can't save *anybody*—anybody but the most important rescue you can make: of yourself, that is.

TWO

Rushmore (Acting)

I wrote a hit play—so I'm not sweating it, either.

—Max Fischer

That the predominant theme of the opening of *Rushmore* is *difficulty*, and the fact, as we soon learn, that it's all a *dream*, this scene, a trompe l'oeil, a literal day dream and in chapel no less (because Max is overtired from working so hard to excel at everything but schoolwork), tells us that this is a movie about several things. But the thing that it's about most is this: the self-referential best and worst of Hollywood. Hollywood, where art meets commerce and brings a community together (just like what Max's "best play ever" will do at the end of the film). Tinseltown, where it's very, very hard to achieve, realize, or even define or keep straight your dreams. Ask anyone who lives here/there. There where *sic transit gloria*.

Ask Wes Anderson. Late in the film, Max lets fall that he couldn't get his "best play ever, man" (as Mr. LittleJeans dubs it) *made* over at Rushmore— like a real director who's had trouble with "the big studio system." Ask Wes Anderson. Ask almost any auteur whose scripts are word-driven. Hence we're back in the familiar and quite fertile realm of self-reflexivity, a notion that's corroborated by the first shots—of a painting, of an unhappy family (cf. Tolstoy and the grand opening of *Anna Karenina*, how "all happy families are alike," but "each unhappy family is unhappy in its own way"), behind a curtain, a richly red and presumably theatrical one to serve as an accoutrement to Max's artist/writer/director-*manque* avocation. What's behind this curtain? Another curtain. Another "thrust into the abyss." What's behind any curtain? Why suspense, and suspense stories, of course— ones which will doubtless require us to suspend our disbelief. The teacher in the initial scene teases about then deflects the preps' interest in "probably the hardest geometry equation in the world." A gauntlet cavalierly thrown. Then picked up by the most unlikely lad. Max, in his dreams, and in dreams alone (save for a few of the littler preppies who follow him, worship him, whom he can control till the curtain of his wizardry is pulled back and they see him for the liar/betrayer he unfortunately is), is a hero—and a spectacularly misguided one. This is a kid who is *dreaming*, as in superlatively deluded—*you're dreaming*, we tell someone who's just disclosed a preposterous ambition or goal. Max dreams not only of getting out of having to do hard work, but also of accomplishing the same for his thankful if not fawning following. A brace-face and pipsqueak who, in reveries, and in reveries alone, is a positive Olympian, carried on the grateful shoulders of his many minions.

Traversing the well-funded classroom, the camera finds the massy blackboard, beautifully adorned with calligraphic equations that might've been etched by a more meticulous Twombly. "Don't worry about that problem," teacher tells a student. Max is already ahead of the class: there are no tangible problems *he's* worried about, problems that count, that'd help bring up his abysmal GPA. Max has that covered—even in dreams. The (impossible) dream reward is that, if anyone can solve "that problem," the MIT-product would, like Max later on hopes to do, "pull some strings with administration" and "see to it none of you would ever have to open another math book for the rest of your lives." An ignominious dream to have. Hardly on a par with saving Latin. Plus ridiculous: even if he wanted to, the teacher couldn't guarantee or see to it. Yet those of us arty-lit types who hated math, a subject that caused us untold worries and stress in school, would've welcomed, and then some, such an odd nerd-hero. And, in the dream, Max's dream is shared by someone—a superior. How lonely and alone he must be/feel. There's a bit of Max in all of us—way back when, or even now. He's an everyman, and one in reverse. God, you wouldn't want to be him—and yet he's us, an everyMax. The worst of us, that is. Perhaps that's why he makes us so uncomfortable when we first meet/meet up with him. Goofy, dorky, smarmy, obsequious, pretentious, selfish, sarcastic, puerile, mendacious, vain, fatuous, manipulative, falsely humble, histrionic, proud, petulant, "big show, no results" (as Buchan observes), *average*, untrustworthy, rude, uncouth, calumniating, opportunistic, with repugnant braces on his teeth and an irrepressible lust for MILFs in his heart— how might redemption ever find him, redeem him, provide us (and Max himself) in the process with any semblance of a happy ending? There's much that's, actually, villainous about this short-arse of a loser-hero. He's, to paraphrase poor wonderful Dr. Guggenheim, one of the *worst* students Rushmore's got. On so many levels.

Levels. This film has as many as do folds in the curtains that figure so prominently. The figure in the curtain, not carpet—not to put too punning a Jamesian point on it.

With its pizzicato accompaniment, the very first shot is of an eponymous, self-reflexive RUSHMORE *sign*. The word within the title. Harking back to something American and difficult, the monumental monument, a paean to greatness, the statues of stature Max improbably aspires to without any of the arduous diligence required to build such a thing, not just dream it up.

Jane Austen famously said of one of her greatest creations—the eponymous Emma from *Emma*—that she knew she'd created a figure her readers mightn't like, wouldn't, most likely, like. Not at first, at least. Many's the moviegoer who's averred that the first or even second times she or he saw *Rushmore* they *hated* it, and hated Max himself. *Hated* the film. Not just didn't like it. When he first comes into view Max is the only one who's got his Rushmore sport/team/school coat on—he's "different," his clothes "announce;" he's true blue, truer than true to the school that's given him a laughable and sentimental "academic scholarship." "I'm on scholarship—academic scholarship," he brags didactically-laughably-ambiguously to breathtaking Miss Cross on the bleachers, lest she'd mistake this scrawny, spotty four-eyes for someone with a sports or arts ride or something. Ha!

The oft-noted/much-derided Andersonian hypermeticulous attention-to-detail is way on display in this first scene. Are those reprints of Jacques Henri Lartigue behind Max's desk? Lartigue with his preoccupations with oddball action and race cars, grown-up versions of the the go-carts Max races round in as a part of the Yankee Racers. Max's desk tells us heaps—film as narrative/filler-in of background story. His overly ambitious character is represented in the Financial section of the newspaper he reads and presumably "annotates." His cosmopolitan/worldly aspirations and pretentions manifested in the crude doodle of the Eiffel Tower, the work of an architectural genius—he *is* president of the French Club, after all, improbably again, as his scores in that subject are sixty-nine, still a "D." There's a calculator for his many calculations, as it were. A cup of espresso for sophisticated refreshment and maximum stimulation (he hasn't been paying attention, even in his reverie, to what the teacher's been saying) in case he needs to spring into action and breezily solve the hardest problems in the world, a world he really only dreams about, not tries to thrive or even minorly succeed in.

"Did someone say my name?" he *ah-ha-ha-ha*'s, knowingly, expecting the call to rush in and save the day, a cool customer, expecting too the imaginary susurrus of excitement at the prospect of others watching him in academic/heroic action. Which is rich: kids his own age either have no idea who he is or, like Buchan, despise him for a phony and dork. "Max Fischer?" Donny scoffs, after he's shoved Max aside to the point where he falls, getting into his dad's Rolls, having lost a tussle for "shotgun" with Ronny, saying Max's name with uber-contempt when Mr. Blume asks if that kid's been invited to "the twins'" birthday party. "Come on, dad, there's gonna be *girls* there," Ronny says, tag-teaming his dad with his gruesome brother's impish help as the car's air conditioning gets turned up to cool down hot-under-the-collar dad; or most likely just to vex him. Max is "known," but only as a loser and Poindexter, popular for his unpopularity with his peers, denigrated perhaps because only the little kids, who don't know better, think he's hot shit and not a dweeb. A stately, dramatic guitar raga gives way to accelerando flutes as Max writes on the board, a Walter Mittyish teacher himself now, tolerantly reversing roles now, pacifically instructing the instructor on how to do it, with his beautifully calligraphic penmanship, calligraphy being another perfect metaphor for Max's flimsy-spurious accomplishments and achievements: they look good *on paper* but they're merely ornamental, "all show, no result." "You did it," Mr. Adams (Dipak Pallana, nice to see you again) praises do-nothing, do-all-the-wrong-things-avidly, the things that don't count, Max. The organ in the soundtrack piece here even mimes/makes a *wow!* sound as Max's classmates hoist him shoulder high, chanting "Fischer, Fischer!" like triumphing warriors or champion sporto's.

We must pay careful attention, and careful attention to detail, while watching this film. The first time you see it you might not know that the opening's a fantasy, something that's only "happened" in Max's head. Segue to the chapel scene and the camera hovers above Max, like a deus ex machina that only occurs in mythology and in the movies, as he wakes up, knackered again, catching catch-as-catch-can up on his sleep as he's so tired from engaging in, as Dr. Guggenheim puts it later, "too many extracurriculars, not enough studying."

(What are Guggenheim's dogs—Nicholas and Copernicus—doing in a church, sitting next to him? What kind of school *is* this? A Richie Rich one, where the headmaster does whatever he wants, waxes as eccentric as he can.) The real, not imaginarily forecasted applause, we find, we hear, is for a guest speaker, not Max. A man of wealth and distinction. And taste? Like a good, attentive student might Max hushes Dirk Calloway—but Max is most likely only interested in poaching whatever he can from this apparent success story of a person, an "important" man, one who looks the part, at least. The shot of his typed-up speech (yet another reflexive example of *writing* in Anderson's films), most likely clacked out by his well-paid secretary, tells us about Blume—all we need to know for now: his own name's on his stationery, an eponymous company name: Blume International. *International*, no less. Steel, we'll later find out. Something strong as strong can be. In theory, that is.

Why is it that the incomparable Bill Murray can do no wrong? In cinema, that is. Having anyone else, any other actor, play Mr. Blume— inconceivable. (The greatest non-pro movie review I have ever heard is this, a one-sentence assessment of Sofia Coppola's *Lost in Translation*, courtesy of my friend Scott Taylor: "Here's my review: 'Rich girl gets Bill Murray.'") With his rich brown not-preppy jacket, shirt, and tie, his somewhat preppy reading glasses (I think they might be the same as Max's), and his thundering intoning from the pulpit, Murray's perfect. And the impression he makes on Max is formidable, indelible, astounding, as is logged by Max (comically, sacrilegiously) in one of the hymnals (with a calligraphy pen, of course):

MAX (his writing): *Rushmore—best school in country rich kids—<u>bad</u>?*
this guy—best chapel speaker I have ever heard

The speaker speaks to Max, to his very core, for the specious advice that hits home: "Take dead aim on the rich boys. Get them in the crosshairs, and take them down." How can Max, ostracized and ridiculed by the rich boys, not like *that*? The speech is too good, too funny not to quote in its entirety:

MR. BLUME—*You guys have it real easy. I never had it like this where I grew up. But I send my kids here because the fact is you go to one of the best schools in the country— Rushmore. Now for some of you, it doesn't matter: you were born rich and you're going to stay rich. But here's my advice to the rest of you: take dead aim on the rich*

boys. Get them in the crosshairs and take them down.
Just remember: they can buy anything but they can't buy
backbone. Don't let them forget that. Thank you.

Max, significantly, is the only one who stands
and claps, a standing ovation of one, solo, a "man"
alone. Max is the only one Mr. Blume's spoken to,
spoken for, we gather. What a character—what
a couple of them. Mr. Blume, self-referentially
speaking, *has* just taken "dead aim on the rich
boys," though "these little pricks," as, walking
away, he refers to them, will hardly be fazed by
his homily/jeremiad/anti-benediction. Max,
however, "translates" Blume's speech for his own
self-aggrandizing devices; Blume didn't say that
Rushmore is *the* best school in the country, but
that's what Max writes down. People hear what
they wanna hear. Max goes to the best school in the
country, one that ostensibly produces extraordinary
"men," like the men and lives Jacques-Yves Cousteau
writes about that Max finds in the book on the
life aquatic that "leads" him to Miss Cross and his
fate. Max *is* an extraordinary "man"—he *must* be.
A prophetic prophet's just told him that. Max has
no idea who "this guy" is, but he certainly does
twig that a spiritual father and brother and kindred
spirit's just given him his blessing to go ahead and do

what he, as an underprivileged student and pariah,
has been longing to do all along: get revenge, albeit
kiddie revenge. (Let us note here that *Rushmore*
might be said to be a revenge comedy, not tragedy,
a sort of new genre—for the quest for getting back
at someone is really going to get out of hand later
on as Max and Blume become bitter rivals for a
spell as they compete for the favors of the same
chick; Blume, ironically, is going to *engineer* his own
"downfall"—but that's what all of us do, anyway,
isn't it? This is one of Anderson's classic themes,
existential hamartia, and it's ours, as well.)

But the *problem* is that Mr. Blume already
has two sons, two whom "never" in "his life"
did he think he'd have sons like, to phrase things
mimetically awkwardly. Terrors, horrors, thrashers,
goons: redheaded neo-Roundheads with a thirst for
violence that's troped by the gross, revolting sport
they excel at, wrestling, and the birthday present
they covet and share, a crossbow—medieval
weapon of destruction for sport and war. (I
remember Anderson noting somewhere that the
kids who play Ronny and Donny are kinda really
like that in real life—the kind of kids who'd snap
a wet towel at your ass in high school.) Blume's
unhappiness and disillusion has been heralded

anyway by the *portrait* at the beginning of the *picture*. He sits, frowning and smoking, while his wife stands above him, arms *crossed*, defensive, closed off, the boys flanking his left: doubles of each other, the living embodiments of self-reflexivity come to life, they're smiling, well, ghoulishly— which can't be good, given what they'd likely smile at. The glee with which Ronny and Donny unwrap that crossbow (as Mrs. Blume surreptitiously flirts with the tennis pro, feeds him birthday cake) is indicative of how low Blume's sunk, and why he'd do his best Benjamin in *The Graduate* and dive to the bottom, smoke and drink in hand, from the diving board, pulling off an obnoxious, puerile cannonball (it may as well have been a bellyflop), trying to get attention in all the wrong ways, make a splash as others "pay" for his misery, get it sprayed in their faces. Blume isn't a man, not really. Not yet. He wears big old shorts with "Budweiser" cheaply emblazoned on them to show how he doesn't come from money but from those who "down" American swill, King of Beers (but he's not king of his own castle, seemingly). He drinks *and how*. He asks Max what the secret is—"You seem to have it all figured out." He asks *a fifteen-year-old fuck-up* for advice. Max's surprised response is both good and bad: "Gee, I don't know. I think it's finding something you love and doing it for the rest of your life—for me it's going to Rushmore." Finding something you love—good. Going to prep school the rest of your life—bad, pathetic.

As the little party walks away from the chapel speech and Herman sparks a fresh Chesterfield, one he might need after such an unnerving if not just merely nervy experience, Dr. Guggenheim chastises, waxes sarcastic, while Max looks around meditatively and flatters Blume: "I thought your speech was excellent," he says banally. And Blume, lost as hell, is touched; he's been recognized, he's gotten through to someone, anyone. There's no getting through, he must figure and in a less-than-admirable and defeatist way, to the twins or to his wife: it's too late, they're toast. But this kid: "Sharp little guy."

"He's one of the worst students we've got."

The dismay and incredulity on Dr. G's face as the camera does a close-up.

Cue the music-video-within-a-movie (mise en abyme encore) montage of the reason why Max is so bad—he's having fun, way too much fun. To the tune of The Creation's "Making Time" (in Max's case—wasting it; and thank Anderson for getting this great, little-known sixties band from Hertfordshire some recognition), we learn some more about Max and his interests and activities. The year*book*, where such thing'll be chronicled, sentimentally made into nostalgic facts. He's the *publisher* of the Rushmore yearbook—big bright letters tell us so as he walks along the leafy grounds with "his" staff, pointing, avuncular, leading people, directing them. French Club president—smiling in the lavish Language Lab with a red beret while everyone else sports a different beret; why are they smiling? French is no smiling matter. But clubs are. Clubs are just for fun. They're not serious business. That any college or university takes your clubs involvement seriously is one of the jokes of American academia. Model United Nations (Russia)—of course Russia, the "bad" guy. (Max wears many hats, as it were and literally here. Funny hats. Though his plight and imminent getting-kicked-out is no laughing matter.) Stamp and Coin Club president—nerd city. What the dickens did anyone ever *learn* from such childish activities? They're pastimes for bored kids with nothing better to do. A stamp or coin collection one collects so that it can collect dust on a shelf somewhere. Debate Team captain—where Max, with Dirk on/by his side, seems to lose it, lose his cool, a harbinger of not-good events to come. Lacrosse Team manager—the preppiest sport, Holden Caulfied bait (in *The Catcher in the Rye*, equipment manager Holden loses all the goddam foils on the goddam subway, you'll recall). Calligraphy Club president—what the hell? Astronomy Society founder—of course Max, a "star," must concern himself with the stars, destiny, stargazing, but not the science behind it/them. Fencing Team captain—ibid., nerdly, fake or mock fighting, a total *individual* sport, historic, theatrical. Track and Field, JV Decathalon—Homeric, heroic, Max jogging along alone, presumably in last place. Second Chorale choirmaster—directing again, waving a baton, the easiest job (to fake) in the orchestra. Bombardment Society founder— now we're talking: "You! You're out," Max gets to gloat as he takes dead aim on a rich boy. Kung Fu Club (yellow belt)—the color of cowardice. Trap and Skeet Club founder—how much funding *is* there at this bloody school? Rushmore Beekeepers president—ditto. Yankee Racers founder—ditto ditto. Max Fischer Players director—making a "name" for himself, holding a skull, "Alas! Poor Yorick." And to crown all, Piper Club, four and a half hours logged—for heaven's sake.

The Creation classic, as good as any early Kinks or Who song, has to do with *shooting lines / for people*

to believe in / things you say / gone in a day and *tellin'
lies / closin' your eyes / makin' more excuses* and
lookin' for / an open door / never taking chances—
Maxy all the way, an ensign-anthem for a guy who
wants to do the same old thing, sing the same old
song, as the song says, for the rest of his life. "His"
theme song, this. But he's biding it, squandering it,
time. Ironically.

The art-ref'd next chapter/curtain comes
as "September." Dr. G's office and an imminent
scolding/schooling's afoot. "Sudden Death Academic
Probation," is Max's status now. Are there cool
echoes of *Animal House*'s "double secret probation"
for the out-of-control Delta House? Scrambling,
waffling, bamboozling, bullshitting, Max asks if he
can "see some documentation on that." He acts like
a grown-up but he's out of his league, his element.
His hands folded piously, a total charlatan, Max tries
to turn the tables. Dr. G, with his professorial pipe
and a portrait of Winston Churchill on the wall, on
his side, isn't having it: "Can't do it, Max," he says,
turning down flat the boy's request for a pass, for
"old time's sake." Max even tries to winkle a "post-
graduate year" at the school he loves so much but
not so well. No go. "We don't offer it *yet*," Max
throws up effetely, begging on behalf of solidarity.
No way. "Just bring up the grades." Max obviously

thinks in terms of possibilities, positively. And positively wrongly directed. He's a kid with a lot of imagination. Too much imagination. That he puts to "use" comically ineffectually. All he can conceive of, in his present predicament, as he tells Dirk, is to "try and pull some strings in administration." It never crosses his "imaginative" mind that he could actually buckle down and hit the books.

It's in Dr. G's office that we learn of the self-referential provenance of Max's tenure at Rushmore. He wrote a play. He's a playwright. "A little one-act" about Watergate. Even Max, linguistically, stumbles as he recalls it, his play. His pause shows how absurd it would be for anyone, let alone a second grader, to try and encapsulate artistically one of the most complex scams in US history. Rushmore's paying now for Max's education and for its own sentimentality and goodwill toward the community. Max belongs at a remedial or reform school, not a high-powered preppy prep mill. "Do you regret it?" maudlin Max saccharinely asks the doc, appealing to cheap-shot psychology, the personal touch a salesman or business man might try to slip in there, use. Max is only selling himself. The good doctor is understandably tired of being sold something. If Rushmore to the outside world is one of the best schools in the country, to Max it's just a playground, with some random classes to attend and, presumably, sleep through. The Blume speech, and Max's obsequious and public reaction to it, may have been the impetus for Dr. G to take action and start the kicking-out process. In fact, the after-chapel scene puts us in mind of a scene that Max himself might have written: boy wonder, strolling along with faithful sidekick, buoys up lost millionaire, "tells it like it is." Knowingly, sagely, donnish. "I really think you're right about Rushmore," the leaden line in actuality sounds. All flummery, no purport.

Nevertheless, Max has been warned. The writing's on the wall. Latinate: ultimatum. It would be "death" to him to have to leave Rushmore. And it wouldn't, it isn't, as we shall find when later Max learns, in Miss Cross's words, to "make a go of it at Grover Cleveland," the public school he's exiled to, like a tyro epic hero, a school aptly named for one of our worst presidents. Max will survive and even thrive. Rushmore isn't everything. It's the sort of lesson you learn later on, when what you thought was important was only what you thought was important.

"Oh no, not again," Dirk tells Max—and us, concerning Max's academic probation-riddled past. How many lives does a cat or slumming student have?

In the library, where, later, he'll "study" Miss Cross's face, Max is not studying but dreaming over the all-important *Diving for Sunken Treasure* text; he talks school politics with an Asian student, how they're going to cancel Latin in order to "make room for Japanese." The pseudo-traditionalist in Max is outraged. *He* tried to get Latin canceled (because, we figure, it's way too tough for him and his ilk). Some nerve. "It's a dead language, I told them," he platitudinizes. Some argument. Thence comes the shot of the *writing* that Max has seemingly been waiting for all his life, the second "message" he's received in one week: "When one man has the opportunity to lead an extraordinary life, he has no right to keep it to himself." The writing's on the wall, in the book. But instead of *leading* him to lead, the verboten scribbling leads petty Max Fischer to go a-tattling—another superfluous and meddlesome task, not extraordinary. Ignoble, rather. "Why?" the nice priest librarian asks understandably as Max asks to see a list of checker-outers, readying himself to bust someone rather than bust a move to save his academic ass.

Mothersbaugh's harpsicordy music ushers Max toward his love and his destiny, the woman he'll inconclusively treasure and go in pursuit of, disastrously. Miss Cross (the gorgeous, bunny-cute Olivia Williams, in nice jumper and skirt, hair in sexy-prim bun) is a vision—beautiful, kind, English, exotic, Harvard-brilliant, and a good teacher (she's encouraging and sweet: see her marks on the little kids' papers). She's also way inappropriate and out-of-his-league. Not to Max, though. She's *reading* Stevenson's *Kidnapped* to the kids. Another sea story, adventure story. Of treasure like she is/will be. Max, a voyeur now, worse than anyone who defaces a library book, sees but doesn't hear. Too bad. The lesson RLS is delivering in the passage she reads is that both fools and wicked men "get paid in the end." Max is a fool (for love, for glory) and will do something wicked later on (cut Mr. Blume's brakes). He ought to have harkened first. Yet what a siren, what a Circe she is, Miss Cross. No way can we blame him for being thusly instantly smitten, having it bad for her. She's any artist/dreamer/nerd's dreamy dream girl.

Cut to another curtain, velvety blue this time. (Has Anderson got a David Lynch thing going, too?) A stage where players play. Play tough guys, gangsters again, à la *Bottle Rocket*. Max, calm and cool and in control, in his element, directs, is good to the "talent," buys them root beers. He doesn't want one. Is he showing them he doesn't have time to enjoy a soda? Or is it that he can only afford so many and is willing to go without? He's only a barber's son, after all. Now Max, however dully, shines. We're the voyeurs now, watching the eponymous "players." Cue allusions to guys called "Enrique Sanchez" and "bags of cocaine." Serious play—to put it oxymoronically. And not.

If Max can't have Miss Cross ("not yet" is she on offer, a possibility) he can still try for Mrs. Calloway. Here we laugh at him, cry for him. Mrs. *Calloway*? That's the Danish actress Connie Nielsen, one of the most beautiful women in the universe. Are you kidding me? Sophisticated and pseudo-suave Max looks a right fool handing her his "card," complete with extension (for people like him who've overextended themselves—*zing!*) number. How droll. How very. Ridiculous. Max takes a fake interest in Dirk—just to get to Mrs. C. We know this as a student calls Max out on it: "What are you—a lawyer?" Max counters, on the defensive. Max doesn't know Dirk's curriculum; he gets it wrong. Poor Dirk. Mad Max—you're crazy if you think Mrs. Calloway in a million years would ever.

Max goes home, walks, no ride waits for him, on account of his dad's busy working at his barber shop. There, the camera invites us to take in the good old fashioned, chockablock, honest prices on the walls, some LPs, a bit of building block illiteracy: "We Do Shave." Americana to the max. Max gets a haircut; it's a way for father and son to bond. What a nice, kind dad. A bit cluelessly indulgent, however. He dotes on Max, does Bert. Can neither remonstrate with him for the sucky geometry score nor help him. Like son, like father— Bert changes the thirty-seven to an eighty-seven: "You almost got the 'A,'" says he. The world needs dreamers. But it needs tutoring more, sometimes. A mini-realization comes with the "rug rethink," as Martin Amis would put it: Max wonders aloud if he's spending too much time putting on plays and starting up clubs. Yeah, well, duh. Bert's no help. "It's possible," he says. He doesn't want to hurt Max. Max will hurt Max—though neither realizes that just yet. "I should probably be trying harder to score chicks," Max appeals. "That's the only thing anybody really cares about." He's wondering about the world here—but of course misguidedly.

He's wondering what people think is important as opposed to what *is* important. Max will score a chick; he doesn't know that yet, but he will. The right one—Margaret—just not the one he thinks he wants. We'll see her outside the house we see in this scene, a nice girl bringing Max a potted plant for a present—something that will *grow*. He'll shun her. He'll be a cad till he learns better. The sea motif comes into play as Max likens himself to a "ship captain," one who has "been out to sea a long time." Indeed. Adrift, more like. On the verge of shipwreck.

Next scene: Miss Cross and the bleachers—where so much happens, ironically. What's Max doing with a lighter to light her fag? He's ready for anything—save cracking a book? Like a chess piece, a pawn that thinks it's a knight, Max moves himself around the stands, moving in on Miss Cross, by turns a dumb-dumb who mistakes Latin American Policy for Latin and a big shot whose "safety" is Harvard. Powerless, he has a book called *The Powers that Be*. Powerful, she has a book on the sea—an obsession? Later we'll learn that her young husband, graduate of Rushmore, has drowned, the most noble and tragic and romantic and heroic and literary somehow way to die. Max uses the one Latin phrase—*sic transit gloria*—as a kind of pickup line. Unfortunately, it kind of works. She's so broken and lonely that male attention, even from a fifteen-year-old dork in a dubious beret, is welcome. With reservations. Her quotation, about how is nothing sacred?, is something Max knows something about. To him, only Rushmore is sacred. Nothing else deserves much respect—especially an age / class / education barrier like the one that towers between them, he and she.

Infatuated, inspired, a knight needs a grail. The very wrongest grail, in this case, as Max petitions to save Latin, though he, a little Odysseus, tricks the kids into signing (up) for more, harder, more difficult work. What an operator. What does he care if a few of his classmates have to suffer further language-learning headaches so long as he can look good and proper noble to his lady languishing? Buchan calls him a "dotty wee skidmark." Cruel but true. Cue Max's shit-eating grin.

Next up, a wrestling meet. Ughs and grunts and violence. NOT PREPPY AT ALL. NOKD *and* NOCD. People sweating, and in *tank tops*. Horrors! Curtains! Here's where we learn that Blume was in Vietnam, was "in the shit"—just as he is now, metaphorically, in terms of his life choices and facing them. Same day, different "shit." Or not. Now it's Blume's turn to talk about *his* "wildest imagination" and the look on his face narrates all: what truly terrible people my teens, my children are. A dad looks in despair at this son(s) when he sees the worst of himself in him/them. When he feels he's powerless to change what's already unchangeable. "One is what one is, partly at least," Samuel Beckett jokes in *Molloy*. Max lies about *his* father's occupation—a neurosurgeon. What a whopper. One Blume swallows. Why shouldn't he? Max has been hanging round rich kids for yonks, so surely he's picked up a bit of information. Besides, lying, Max is good at it, something easy to do that he's darn good at. Of course he's callow and foolish and insecure, but we can't and shouldn't forgive Max for betraying Bert so. He is that egregious, Hollywoodish thing: a born actor. He's thespianism at its very worst; he's someone who seems to believe his own not just lies but whole roles, whole lives built on fibs and classic mendacity. Like an icy cold glass that "magically" starts sliding across a table, actors are mysterious and slippery and fun to watch. Yet this: "An actor is a guy," Marlon Brando, the best of his generation, famously said, "You ain't talking about *him*, he ain't listenin'." No kidding. Dr. Johnson told Boswell who was in credulous

awe of actors like Johnson's old friend and student
David Garrick (the best of *his* generation) that "a
child of five could play Hamlet." No *kidding*. I'm
with Johnson: it's just mimicking life, getting
the tone right. A kindergartner wouldn't have
to understand the words "'Tis not alone my inky
cloak, good mother, nor customary suits of solemn
black" to pull it off, the Dane. I'm with Hitchcock
who referred to them as cattle. Max the player lies,
acting rather than taking meaningful *action* to save
his Rushmore scholarship, turns down Blume's
kind, charitable invite to the twins' birthday party,
saying he's got a previous engagement. Which
prompts Blume to lose his head and offer Max a
job. But a "job" is already in progress, engaged in,
as Max is shiftily, though he doesn't even know it
yet, going to work (instead of coming to work) on
his elder and better. Rather. The scheme comes to
those who "Iago," as it were. I'm not saying Max is
that bad, anywhere near one of Shakespeare's worst
twist-o's, but bad schemes accompany big dreams
unless they're monitored, supervised wisely. It isn't
likely that Max has read the existentialist Heidegger,
but he might intuit collectively unconsciously that
philosopher's dictum that, "He who thinks great
thoughts, often makes great errors." So many of

the mistakes we make, are making, we don't even
know about, know the nature of, at the time.

Was it a mistake for Herman, too, to give Max
the money to put toward the aquarium he, Max,
"builds" for Miss Cross? Why does Mr. Blume cut
Max a check for twenty-five hundred? Sure, they
get on *en merveille*, they "understand one another,"
like what Miss Cross wants Max to "get." So what,
though? Even in the face of possible death (as Max
confesses later on that he's rigged up a tree to try
and have it fall on Blume), Blume goes: "That
would've flattened me like a pancake," giving Max
credit for nefarious inventiveness. Blume must feel
sorry for the "sharp little guy"—watching him get
his ass thoroughgoingly kicked in record time at
the wrestling match. One of many ass-kickings ass-
kissing Max will get; this one, however, deserving
of a Dignan-like Spirit Award. You know within a
second that the bigger fucker on the rival school
team is going to take Max down soon as you see him
and they shake hands and Max pathetically goes,
"Nice to see you again." "Be true to your school,"
the stupid old song goes "just like you would to
your girl or guy." Max doesn't have a girl, so he picks
his school to be true to. Rushmore's his Rushmore
("She was my Rushmore," he tells Blume after the

tree fails to fall, fails to take Max's worst-instincts-indicative direction) before Rosemary becomes it, his Rushmore. And Miss Cross becomes, as in is very becoming of it, his obsession, in her comely fashion. Becomes Blume's, too, a dream (girl) they share and don't/won't.

Re: the aquarium. Just look how excited he is! "Piranha? Really?" That should've been a red flag right there. Talking the talk leads to walking the walk and vice versa. A real, if bizarre, friendship's formed. All boyish joys recapitulated, relived for Blume, experienced anew too for Max. Max's "thing" with Mr. Blume's just the flipside of him hanging around primarily with the little preps. Popping wheelies, taking the juniors on field trips in packed vans, playing tennis at the club with Miss Cross, going out to a lavish dinner after Max's first "hit play," Max and Blume hit it off, little knowing what's (who's) to come/get, between them.

Let's talk about her for a bit. She who must be not-obeyed. Rosemary, slightly self-conscious about her name (as Herman, understandably is his), hasn't had it easy. Being a widow's resulted in loneliness, dedication to her job, and a curious "thing" for fish—her husband's "thing" (she's not going to get into beekeeping, that'd be just plain weird, and dangerous). Fish-collecting, aquaria, are for people who like to *watch*, sit in the bleachers, not get involved, sit this one out, not participate, not have to do a lot of work like what you have to do with a dog for a pet. Miss Cross has, obviously, been on the sidelines too long. When Blume comes courting, she's home alone in her ex's vast cold sad house, having a melancholy carrot after school like a good girl. One who, maybe, is dead sick of being good, who yearns secretly to be a naughty girl, find a fellow, as Dirk naïvely notes in his tattletale break up letter to Max, so they can go "giving each other hand jobs" poolside, "meet someone" and go to bed with him, despite the fact that she seems to be a bit in love with being lonely. She does after all have an affair with a married man. She does after all (after all he's done) kick Max's ass, or at least put him on it, which is all that he deserves. Something scandalous and salacious in a Wes Anderson joint! She's not a flat character, nor a Goody Two–shoes. She's a real person, kind of a badass, Ivy League version, never an actress-in-life, and a glorious person at that. Part of why Miss Cross is so endearing and human and real is that she can't help herself, either. With respect to the Max thing. She knows. And she knows she knows. And there's no stopping some people—sometimes even when those people are oneself. The human thing. Ultra self-referential. She knows she's "let him get too attached," as she tremulously confesses to Blume as a little kid, *painting a painting*, says, "That's a...that's a jellyfish." My favorite line. Fish again. Fischer. "Max, has it ever crossed your mind that you're far too young for me?" Rosemary sternly but conspiratorially whispers, a sexy honorary librarian, as Max sharpens Freudian pencils, sweetens her up with bottomless glasses of lemonade. Her dewy look here betrays her, and badly. She's touched. Her eyes are watering. She's seen the way he gazes at her lips, listened to him be concerned that she's a smoker, received his presents (more fish) and his blandishments, heard about his efforts on behalf of Latin and the Rushmore aquarium, heard him sandwich in forced connections between the two of them ("I guess we both have dead people in our family," Max says weirdly, straining, after she points out, "These were just born." Just born like their "love.") What a shock and a drag to find she's married (as Max drops the fishnet into the tank); what a relief to learn her husband's dead. If only he wasn't a child, she maybe figures. And "such a child." She's *well* flattered. She falls for the oldest trick in the book: being told (by Max) that he's "never met anyone like" her. A feeling she, rather disastrously, reciprocates, not aware of how ready to become a monster-of-love Max's ego/hopes is/are. Realizing at dinner that Max, making a terrible scene, insulting her doctor/Harvard friend Peter, "scoring" off him with the immortal, *"Oh, are they?"* comeback to learning that Peter's in "OR scrubs," has at last gone too far. "And I'm in love with you!" he sighs way dramatically, punctuating in neon and glitter the fact that he's kind of, well, bonkers. Love can drive one crazy, in the good crazy way, Anderson seems to say, but it can make one mental too. And *en guarde* when it comes to *cherchez la femme*! Rosemary tries to deflect Max's wooings but he's already made up "their" story. "Neither of us knows where this relationship is going," he avers. She counters that stance with logic, tells him they don't *have* a relationship. Love v. logic—good luck with that. He isn't having it. *Au contraire*! He has an answer for and to her every objection, even (ironically) threatening to "grab a dictionary" and get the *author*ities involved. Max is already entitled. Entitled to be her *cavalier servente*. It's no use resisting this. It's love. It's real. If he believes it, it's got to be. He's a bit of a romantic sociopath. He's just a kid. Kids say the darndest things, and do and think the most demented. "I understand. You're not attracted to me," Max pouts. He knows that that attraction, unlike the age difference, can change, has changed between women and men from time immemorial. The conversation Max is "glad we had" (he's great at turning the tables on people) ends in a handshake again. The handshake motif. He's gotten one off of Mrs. Calloway, but this is different. The hand*shake* concept must've lead, by a sort of linguistic association of ideas, to the fateful, slanderous one about the hand *job*.

Still, Max must walk away still in hope here; after all, she's never met anyone like him either. That's enough to go (deludedly) on for now.

One of the most beautiful things about this beautiful and extraordinary film is how often one character helps another to see who he or she really is, where he or she went wrong. Such is the case for sure with Rosemary, whom Max, near the end, calls out for being still in love with a dead guy, just when she tries to queen it over him and Herman about how Edward Appleby's "got more spark in one fingernail than..." "One dead fingernail," Max parries. "I mean, you live in his room, with all his stuff..." he says. Time for her to grow up, grow out of grandiosely living in the unlivable past. "He hates himself," Miss Cross says of Mr. Blume, but maybe, deep down, Max, trucing at last, senses that if he matchmakes instead of cockblocks he, Blume, his former friend and friend again, maybe won't hate himself anymore, be the sort of man who swats a little kid's lay-up just for fun and to make himself feel better. Do you have any idea how funny it is to block a little kid's shot like that—to the swatter? It's great good not-grown-up fun, let me tell you. Do it once—very funny. Keep it up, you're not any kind of amusing.

Back to Blume. After the wrestling, there's the birthday party. More scoring—as in getting presents. Anderson gives us the impression that Blume could've used a friend there, is missing little Fischer, as he tipsy-bored throws golf balls into the pool and doesn't give "a rat's ass," like what he says to some guy on the phone at work. Herman's obviously lost his lust for life, has no pep in his step. He's suffering from ennui and it's dangerous, too. Maybe looking to get back in the shit again—shit he's already *in* so fuck it, what the fuck! "Met a girl, fell in love, glad as I can be," Ray Davies of Anderson's beloved Kinks sings over sad, tinkling acoustic guitars as the pool scene begins and Mrs. Blume steps over the line, looks around guiltily, with the tennis pro. We all know how that song turns out: "But I think all the time 'Is she true to me?'" it goes. Sexual jealousy— the eventuality of love triangles like the sexual geometry that's materializing between Blume, Miss Cross, and Max. On the diving board, Mr. Blume gets attention, practically demands it...gets attention in the wrong way, the not-good-for-him psychological way. Everybody stops and gawks. Is he wasted? Does it matter? He looks like a guy who thinks he's wasted his life, his time, his talent, his genius, his empathy. The little kid swimming is understandably afraid of him, huddled to himself, hugging himself, at the bottom of the deep end. This is Benjamin had he stayed with Elaine (you know Ben and Elaine split up, right?)

Speaking of films, and film, the scenes within the scenes, Max's theatrical plays (things you "put on"—like people) and the self-referential element of the fact that *Rushmore* is the story or portrait of an artist-(manqué) as a young man (or fool). *Serpico* and *Apocalypse Now* get the Maximum pastiche treatment, wonderfully parodied, though Max is too inexperienced and hampered by his own vaulting confidence and the praise of others not to think he's an original. And he is. Kind of. Anderson may have and rightly resisted the temptation to use the overt "I'm Not Like Everybody Else" Kinks song. Speaking of music, The Dream Syndicate, say, a Paisley Underground band from the short-lived eighties LA scene, and

Luna, the nineties spin-off of Galaxie 500, are both total rip-offs of the Velvet Underground, but they've got something, in spite of their unabashed thievery, that's still much their very own. Jeff Lynne's ELO couldn't be more wannaBeatles, but they're great. Don't talk to me about Oasis, however (unless it's to remind me that George Harrison, much to one's own puckish delight, denigrated them, dissed and dismissed them).

"Well, moving on..." as Max says in the bleacher scene, look how excited the entranced little kids sitting at the stage's feet are as the gunshots and shout-outs of the *Serpico* play-homage echo thrillingly. Heroes and tough guys encore. Max takes it all very seriously, like a "real" artist might. Gets in a fistfight (ass kicking once more) with a player who alters a line. "Every line matters," Max pompously, or meticulously, declares. Is Max "Wes Anderson," the director who is more than notorious for taking pains? Well, yeah. On a certain level. If Max is all of us artists and dreamers and Anderson's a dreamer/artist then...sure.

Who could resist such a thunderous curtain call? Not Max. Not us for him. We're hooked now. He's terrific, a boy wonder/*enfant terrible*. Even in his delusions of grandeur. Anderson pumps up the volume, slows down in slow motion the posing as Maxy takes a bow. Well done. For a kid, an amateur in the true sense of the term. It's all done for love anyway. For the sake of a girl. There's very little distance between this show and a real hero's efforts à la Andre Jurieu, the hero of one of Anderson's (and any true blue film buff's) favorite films, Jean Renoir's *La Règle du Jeu*. Hubris and "success" fuck with Max's already-fucked head and he does something, after the show, that's very uncool if not heinous: he lies to Bert about the afte-party being "cast and crew only," and he sniffs at Bert's magnanimous offer of money to cover the fête he "can't" come to.

Max's lies have trapped him and, besides, he has bigger fish to fry: Miss Cross. Whom he's looking around for of course *après* the performance. Crestfallen he is as there *she* is—with a guy. Inconceivable. "How was the slap?" an actor asks backstage, prefiguring the one Max is about to get "in the face" when he meets handsome Peter, Harvard doctor, just a friend, though Max can't think that that's a possibility on account of who could just be friends, "in a strictly platonic way," with such a babe as his lady love, Miss C? Ouch. How will he handle it, knight-with-imaginary-rival-right-in-front-of-him? Like the child he still is, is how: "Who's this guy?" Appallingly ill-mannered. Where's his St. Anthony to step in and go: "That's just, like, *bad manners*." Max gets a well-deserved and most taboo grown-up whiskey sour (from naughty Blume), and a lesson (courtesy of Miss C) at the celebration dinner. A lesson he doesn't learn, unfortunately. "You're being rude," Rosemary tells him. "I wrote a hit play!" he screeches, thinking immaturely that just because you're an "artist" with "accolades" *you'll get the girl*. Life doesn't work like that. Not outside the movies, it doesn't. And sometimes not even in them. He's not a real artist, not yet, in part because he has yet to realize that, sometimes, *not* getting the girl is better for your art. Most of the time, at least.

Mr. Blume, looking on and helpless as could be, lets his friend hang himself. Or maybe he's just toasted. What can you do? Boys will be boys. We don't get the sense that Blume's scheming scams on Rosemary just yet, but how could he not be interested? The way she's handled Max's outrageous outburst—princessy in a good way. And she *is* right there, all right, right next to him; she already looks the *part* of replacement-wife. He's shy, anyway. Playing hide-and-seek as he comes to deliver Max's calligraphic apology/excuse. He's already more wooer than go-between, hiding behind a tree like a fairy character in *As You Like It*, in awe of R's "way" with kids—a way he maybe used to have. The close-up of her in her *artist's smock* says it all: she's amazing. Here's another guy falling for her as he watches her with kiddies, maternal and caring, plus sexy: "You're both little children," she tells Max in the fake blood/fake bike accident scene. She's only right. "I don't think I should see Max anymore," says she. It's like a break up. She's already looking for someone's approval, that she's done the right thing. "I think you did your best," he tells her, comforting, manly, not drooling but ready to drown in her big gray eyes.

Max's apology is also an invite "to the *unveiling* of a new venture." Curtains again. Like Dignan, he's no quitter. Like Dignan, like Miss Cross and her smoking, he should quit. Not him. Not Max who when he does stuff he does it to the max. Like the groundbreaking ceremony for the phantom aquarium. "Cut the music," Max directs, realizing "she" isn't coming. Enter the "villain," the "evil" Dr. Guggenheim. "Max! What are you doing?" Busted! Tears in the headmaster's office, ominous thunder. Kicked out at last, out on his ass, Dignaned. For the better. One thing good art serves to remind us: you don't know till later. What seems a catastrophe (a Greek word for "an overturning," something real bad for a seafaring people who didn't necessarily teach their sailors to swim before launching them on the Mediterranean) might not be, might be the best thing that's ever happened to you. Art gives us hope: sound and vision versions. If we step back, think, and don't panic. The "betrayal" Miss Cross perpetrates and the fact that she and Blume are both out sick that day bodes ill for our boy, for the film hints that she and he, Herman, are hooking up already, though a tryst for both is long overdue. Max, perhaps intuits this and turns vicious: "Fuck it, I'm building it anyway." "No, you're not" (the line Max uses on Blume re: getting the check). "Tell me this isn't happening," Guggenheim says. Tell me this is a dream. Touché. Max would rather not "have this conversation in front of [his] crew." Film crew, too. For like most narcissists/wannabe artists, he wants "some documentation" on his every move. Did Kubrick ever make a "the making of?" Did Hitchcock or even David Lean? Hardly.

Grover Cleveland and starting over. Though the Rushmore uniform Max hangs on to screams otherwise. He does start by telling the truth, at least—that he's recently been expelled—but he's unflappable, unsinkable, even though his heart (in his voice) sinks as he tells his story, delivers his little autobiography, tells his short saga, like Blume sort of did at chapel—only much different. Now, echoing Blume, but in reverse in a way, Max will take dead aim at the not-rich boys and girls, help them. Help them start up things they have no interest in. A fencing team? Just look at the look on the-kid-in-front's face as Max says that. Being "different" gets him something he's never had: interest from one of the chicks he "ought" to have been trying to score. Margaret Yang is adorable—though Max can't/won't see that. He's still so stuck/fucked-up on Miss Cross that he snubs the little cutie and calls her "Mrs. Chang:" "I'll see you later, Mrs. Chang," he flutes, carrying on with the too-busy persona that worked for him at his old school. We love that line, that touch. She's like him, good old Margaret is: she's not going to quit just because he doesn't see her, just because he doesn't see her yet. Like Max after Blume's speech, she tells him she liked it. Typical Andersonian symmetry and parity. Nice. She uses the same line (almost) Max used on Miss Cross—that she's never heard of anyone like him, giving a speech first day like that. They're both spunky; and moreover they're destined/meant for each other. Though *we* don't know that yet.

In the next scene there's the same sort of symmetry as Mr. Blume looks through a window at Rosemary, just as Max has, earlier, initially, through a door. The lady doth protest too much as Blume tries to talk Max out of liking her, runs her down as "not that beautiful, not that intriguing." Blume swats the little kid's shot just like he swats Max's yearning for Miss C, just like the hall monitoring teacher swats Max's phone call, after the basketball team (playing a pleb sport, one for the masses) swats Max (fencing with no one) out of the gym. Max goes back to where he once (sort of) belonged—Rushmore—only to find Buchan like a Puck/Caliban up in a tree, gloating and calling Max out for a fucking liar, for making up stuff about "getting a hand job in the back of a Jaguar" from Mrs. Calloway. A happier encounter with Miss Cross—with a prop Max uses to show her he's got something on her (the Cousteau book). It "works" in that it occasions Rosemary telling Max he reminds her of her late husband. Good intentions, big mistake. They talk by her car, like lovers fencing over whether they should "make a go of it" again. He doesn't even seem to notice she's around five feet taller than he is. He proposes…friendship. And tutoring. "Do you think we can be friends again—in a strictly platonic way?" he pleonasms. Ha! Chicks dig guys who dug them, lose them, still want to be friends with them.

Cheerleading, getting plays going again, doing better in math, Max is *mad* ripping it up. Everybody's having fun. On a "group date" there's Dirk, between Rosemary and Herman as they check out some hoops. Plucky Margaret's back for more, wants a role: "And bring a headshot," Max tells her. Another line, another obvious nod to the movies. And another reminder of Max's incorrigible conception of himself as greater, more glorious than he is. A headshot for a high school play? Gimme a break. But that's Max. And no matter how much they change, people really are relentlessly themselves, don't you know.

The ruse Blume pulls on Rosemary, turning up faking that Max had something planned for them. Not this. A romantic walk. And so it begins. Holding hands. But Dirk sees them, busts Blume. "I know about you and the teacher," he says ponderously, officiously, like he's a character in one of Max's plays. "With friends like you who needs friends," the line goes. Friendship motif. "Fischer ain't your mate," Buchan tattles. Dirk knows the truth about his "friend," that Buchan's right—he's standing up for the wrong guy. Betrayal begets betrayal, and so Dirk does some writing of his own: a cinematic letter that lets Max know he's no "pal" anymore and that Mr. Blume and "the teacher" are fucking/"giving each other hand jobs." "Hurt people hurt people," a good but rather facile line goes in Noah Baumbach's *Greenberg*. No kidding.

A noirish scene with Max, darkly, hiding in the back seat of Blume's car. Blume coming clean. Childishness about who was in love with her first. Hurtful words from former friends—the ones you hurt most. Enter the mayhem. Which begins with Max burning bridges (coming by to tell Miss C that he wants to thank her for "ruining" his life), then leaves out front of Rushmore (flipping off Dr. G), then something serious: telling Mrs. B that Herman's having an affair. On a downtown rooftop like what might happen in a Scorsese, Mrs. B talking/acting tough in a headscarf like a moll in disguise; Max, ever the control freak director, has *catered* the affair/ rendezvous himself: tuna fish or peanut butter and jelly? "I'll have the tuna fish," Mrs. Blume sneers. "Get to the point," she commands him: a line that could be a trope for Max's entire aesthetic, the best and most necessary advice he'll ever get. A cinematic siren sounds as he spills the beans, triggering Blume checking in to a hotel, staying indefinitely. Deadly bees from the former beekeeper, and the fight begins. Max has been playing around all his academic life but now he's not playing around. In disguise (a waiter at the hotel), and in filmic slow motion, the brouhaha accelerates, to the great Who tune with the quite-germane-to-the-situation title, "A Quick One While He's Away," that goes *You are forgiven*. With Max trying to put the brakes on Blume's affair (and his very life), things have gone too far and the real cops have gotta be called in. Max is in jail, then bailed out by his real dad. He's gotta go get a teacher fired but even though Dr. G has never taken him for an informer (thought the better of him) he's too late. Miss C has quit. Another ass kicking (and Max falls on his butt, deservedly, in an acorn fight). More quotes from films: "I'm gonna pop a cap in his ass...tell that stupid Mick..." ("He's from Scotland," one of the little kids corrects Max—who doesn't know the difference between a Mick and a Jock.) Max is "trying to win [Miss Cross] back." Wrong. Blackmail, sabotage. Another ass kicking—in Miss Cross's room as she's clearing out her things. Apologies and then he goes too far and tries to kiss her; she loses it, waxes cross, and puts him where he belongs: on his butt. The truth is worse than a thumping, another kind of kicking. "Not if you've ever fucked before," she ruthlessly states to his admonishing her that her deflecting of the possibility of having sex is "a crude way to put it." Buchan comes along to punctuate the scenes with another thumping, a superfluous one. Max dreams on: "We got him, Dirk." Ha!

The film moves swiftly toward its brilliant play-within-a-play conclusion as Max grows (up), realizes "she loves [Blume]" and that she's his Rushmore, too. The Rolling Stones' "I Am Waiting" (an album cut, deep—a great forgotten song by the second greatest band ever) shifts the mood toward good cheer and rapprochement. We're all waiting, holding out, kids, Anderson hints. Max, bitterly, hasn't learned not to hide from those who are meant for him. As Margaret tries to console him with her plant gift. A very lonely montage of sad Thanksgivings: Rosemary alone, Blume eating in his office, Max and Bert with TV dinners. Max is humbled, dropped out of G. Cleveland, a barber's son working in his father's shop. Along comes Dirk to make peace. Offering a Christmas present and getting a haircut like what Bert has given Max. Contrition. A touching scene with a knife like a memento mori from "Sudden Death Academic Probation." Max finds out what a jerk he's been: "You were a real jerk to me," Margaret tells him as Dirk flies a kite, as she flies a toy, not a Piper Cub, but it's good enough for a détente and an introduction to Dirk. Margaret is a fake and overachiever—she fakes a science project. This girl's got potential. They are meant for each other. So alike.

Humiliation leads to humility. It's good like that. Truces beget truces, and Max goes with a plant/flower ("These are glorious"—glory motif) to the hospital to see his old headmaster. "It's Fischer!" Max does good—albeit a comic/ironic sort. Dr. G, in consternation or alarm, snaps out of his mini-coma, haunted by his junior nemesis. "It's Fischer!" Max is waking/shaking things up. For the power of good now. Blume's got *his* ass kicked—by Ronny or Donny, by life and loss (of Cross). Blume and Miss Cross have broken up—and Mr. Blume is "a little bit lonely," i.e. way fucked up. One more ruse and like a lover in a book or movie Max gets in Miss Cross's window with a ladder and a lie about getting hit by a car, using the fake blood from his sets to fake her out as he brings along a tape/ *soundtrack* in order to see why she's dumped Blume and maybe if she might consider…him. A heart-to-heart and more learning and more *lines* ("War does funny things to men.") Max gets busted again—for the fake blood, and at last he must realize he can't get a "very pretty" babe with ruses. He does get the kiss he's lied about and longed for, though. Though that's it. She's had it again—but like a friend, he's helped her to see it's time to bury the past and Appleby. Back out the window. *Au revoir* or *adieu?* We'll see.

Max comes alive as Cat Stevens sings "The Wind." A wind of change. The team's back, "Take dictation, please;" a new play, a new idea from an idea guy like Max. A list of possible cast members. Then a gift to Blume—a pin. He'll take punctuality. Tweedy/twee Anderson at his nerdiest but it's a great, affecting scene that leads to Max really growing, introducing his "father" to his real father, as he really is: a humble barber. A haircut makes the (new) man and Blume, looking sharp and clean cut, is in bloom. Cue the jolliest post-Beatles song: "Oh Yoko!" "We're gonna need all of it," the money Blume has as they, together, will build the aquarium for Rosemary and get her back—for Blume, this time. "She's not coming!" Déjà vu. Max cajoles Blume: "And that's all you're prepared to spend?" Max, symmetrically, goes go-between. "I gave it to my friend," Max tells her, of the idea re: aquarium. He's shared something significant. Max gets dynamite. He's ready to blow up. As an artist. He even makes peace with Buchan, after getting revenge with a pop gun. Then a role for the Scottish kid. Art brings Caliban and tyro-Prospero together. "You wanna be in a play?" Max/Prospero asks.

BUCHAN—*I always wanted to be in one of your fucking plays.*

MAX—*I know you did, mate.*

Curtain for "January"—a new year and a new start and a new play. Max puts everything he knows into this one, all of his suffering and shit. He pulls "a fast one" on Rosemary and Herman, seats them side by side, where they belong, to watch him triumph. The community big and little (the inner circle/triangle) is unified by art. The crew is back together again and the thing's dedicated to Max's mother, and "to Edward Appleby, a friend of a friend"—but it's really for Herman, for Rosemary, for all of us Andersonians, and all the world's a stage and all of us mere players, Max Fischer players or otherwise. Even Bert gets set up—with a proud teacher of Maxy's. Hope and love *do* conquer all. The play brings Max together as well with Margaret—he's got to get something out of it, more than mere recognition and after-party flowers. He deserves a girl. "Get your own partner, Mr. Blume. I'm spoken for," Margaret says, claiming her "man," however aw-shucks he still is about going steady.

The play's the thing wherein we'll catch the conscience/emotional status of some "people" we've come to know and care about greatly. Buchan's not so bad: look how excited he is to be a toy/play soldier; all he needed was to stop being a bully and shooting darts into little preps' necks was his "big break." Mr. LittleJeans, the baseball coach, Peter, the kid from the pool, Bert with popcorn (like a moviegoer and a proud papa: "My son wrote it!"), the Yangs—a super Anderson tracking-shot, a cavalcade of stars as well, the audience, the real stars, we who appreciate and applaud and recognize greatness.

A dance or a wedding—that's how Shakepearean comedies end. You've gotta have one, and this has both—for "Rae Chan" will marry, she says, "Esposito." A dance then, also, after the show, after the "best play ever." Is *Rushmore*, cowritten by Owen Dignan Wilson, Anderson's best film ever?

You tell me. We can talk about it, as the cast does afterward. "That kid's gonna burn this place down," the teacher/hall monitor warns. "You'd better believe it," Herman puns, believing in his friend and his friend's coming into his own as a real artist now. A sort of one, at least.

Acting leads to *action* and reconciliation and celebration. "When the fighting stops…" Max, as "Rambo" in *Apocalypse* says, meaningfully, signaling to lachrymose Blume with a peace sign. The fighting *is* done, between them, a hard fought (for) truce. How all of us want to stop fighting—fighting the wrong people, people we love, our enemies, ourselves. We long to stop *acting,* too, pretending, being phony, being someone we think we should be or we think others think we should be. One last curtain before the final curtain. Max looks dwarfed by his own stage; that's how it should be: he should be smaller than life, smaller than the stage life he's going to bring to life right in front of us. Try if you cannot to be "moved" by what's put so amateurishly (the term evokes love for something) on display. A wry parody of the state of film today, with all the overdone explosions? A minor hitch, with Max getting one last (minor) injury that, momentarily, brings the action to a halt. Intermission and the scene with Blume and Cross outside puts me in mind of Barry going out to the terrace to fetch Lady Lyndon in Kubrick's incomparable masterpiece. Not saying Anderson's derivative here; he just reminds me of things, works of art, that I love. "Works of art beget works of art," Auden or someone said. Yeah, no kidding.

MISS CROSS—*So what do you think of Max's latest opus?*

MR. BLUME—*It's good. But let's hope it has a happy ending.*

Opus? Oh, *really?* He has arrived, Max has. And so have all the lovers, and so have we who love cinema. The hopeful "Semper Fi," is our exit line, along with and more important than sadder *sic transit gloria.* Max tears a page/tagline from the script of his own experience. And maybe, just maybe, he truly understands its purport; maybe he's not just mouthing it now, he knows, he's learned.

In comes the pool kid with a sparkler—the sparkler from *Bottle Rocket*? Haha! Mise en abyme again and double-self-reflexively. Sparks are flying. Celebration time.

Max tells Miss Cross, "I didn't get hurt that bad," meaning more than in just the production. How big he's "grown." How magnanimous of him to have said that. It's like what a real hero would say, in or out of the movies. We can relax about Max, and still laugh at how he's still pulling strings, not just the ones backstage, the ones his marionettes proffer, how he's getting the production past obstacles, by some conniving way or another as a few dissenting voices of some huggermuggering teachers whinge about how he's not doing stuff according to code, according to "the system." How relieved we are that one can change and not change *too* much, still be one's essential self. And how Max deserves one last dance with his old "flame," Miss Cross. She takes his glasses off: now that he can *see*, now that he's no total geek/nerd/dweeb but an artist/hero/human success story, he's got no need for those clunky black Clark Kents; now that he needn't hide behind the brainiac/pretentious-art-guy front those trademark specs have somehow signified.

As a fare-thee-well Anderson gifts us one more sixties classic meant to travel straight up our spines: The Faces's big number, "Ooh La La," a song about wishing we knew when we were younger what we know now. A rousing, fitting, monumental soundtrack to the soundtrack of Rushmore's and *Rushmore's* characters' lives.

Ooh, la, la. And how.

Curtain.

THREE

The Royal Tenenbaums *(Being)*

You didn't even have to think about it.

—Eli Cash

Like with respect to the wages of sin, prodigy exacts a price, one over and above the obvious one of the prodigious one's lost (in both senses of the term) childhood. Chas, Margot, and Richie Tenenbaum in Anderson's *The Royal Tenenbaums* are each perverted somehow; they're monsters all. Not horrible ones, but monsters in the sense that the Middle English word "prodigy" derives from *prodigum*, Latin for monster and omen. Chas is a workaholic and an unforgiving control freak, Margot secretive and promiscuous and unfaithful, Richie addicted to melancholy and lovesickness for his adopted sister. We realize how preposterous and improbable such beings are (there are no *real* child prodigies in business, literature, and sport: the only fields baby geniuses *can* occupy are music and mathematics, on account of it doesn't take any life experience to conjure up the music of the spheres and write, say, a symphony of Mozartian proportions, or to solve some difficult equation when the little kid in question somehow and inexplicably just "sees" the answer). None of the trinity of Tenenbaum whiz kids can have existed; they're purely fictional, so we needn't be too concerned for them. This film is a fairy tale within a fairy tale, a self-referential dream of an ur-story already dreamed up by a weaver of webs for children of all ages in that the Tens's resemblance to J. D. Salinger's mythopoeic Glass family is all too apparent and self-consciously so. This film, speaking of debts and prices, owes a regular leprechaun's pot o' gold to literature itself, and in specific to the god of fucked-up, fascinating, preppy-genius families: the eccentric superpreppy recluse who wrote *Franny and Zooey* and *Seymour: An Introduction* and The Big One that fucked him majorly up 'cause he got too famous for it (read for the pun) and started freaking out about Being and Nothingness and Buddhism and all that stuff. The American sensation who became even more famous for not wanting to be famous anymore, notoriety following him around, haunting him, rendering him the quarry of so many lost autograph/wisdom-hunters, people in search of a goddam Jerry Salinger who didn't exist, as it were, anymore. The first shot we get is of the book *The Royal Tenenbaums*—which saves us some trouble already 'cause we can just see the film (which *is* the book, which "is" *a* book) instead.

Over wafting-lovely never-never land harp music the title (as in book title) within the title appears. Anderson appears to be addicted to boxes within boxes—*mise en abyme* yet again. In a way, it's good that his team couldn't get the original of the opening number, "Hey Jude," a to say the least transcendental/fucking amazing song about a lost kid who needs consoling for an absent parent; it's good that it's a cover, a fake or "fugazi" in the slang sense, in that were this family and their story of "failure, betrayal, and disaster" "*real*" and/or realistically portrayed, it'd be way too much for us to take, an act that'd overwhelm us, and not necessarily in a good way. So it, the film, takes a sad "song" and makes it "better" by making it style-heavy, too beautiful for words, the kind of work of art that got critics going grousing that Anderson was turning not only into an aesthete—all style, no substance—but also in on himself, becoming a solipsist's solipsist, practicing art for his own sake.

(Richie, Wes's alter alter-ego, does take a selfie, an indulgent *autoportrait*, when we first meet him, after all, on the *Cote d'Ivoire*.) Seen this way, as pure and intentional pastiche, we can forgive *The Royal Tenenbaums* its many flaws, its precious preciousness. For it's still a big film about big things: forgiveness and the question of Being in particular. What are we to do with (the story of) our lives? How much of it is fake, how much real? Who are we now, who were we, what will we be?

All you need is love, the Beatles theorized, insisted. But what if those you need to love are unlovable, selfish beasts, charming but truly destructive? Regal Royal's a royal bullshitter, as all good (and all disbarred) lawyers are. He's a king who lives in a palace, The Lindberg Palace. But a king-in-exile, saddest of the sad, "out on his ass," à la Dignan and Max; and the palace he's thrown out of is named for a hero / "betrayer." A fraud of a dad, a con man, asshole, traitor ("There are no teams!" he schools Chas during the BB gun fight), Royal's one of Anderson's greatest liars and a real not wannabe thief (he's stolen his children's childhoods and their love, plus "bonds out of [Chas's] safety deposit box when [he] was fourteen"), a rogue royale. Only after he speaks does he realize that what he's said is true, that he means it. One of the coolest lines of the film comes as Royal's kicked out of "his" own house, busted by Mr. Sherman for doing the unthinkable, faking having cancer so that he can serve his own ends: "I know I'm gonna be the bad guy on this one. But I just want to say that the last six days [of convalescing and having fun with the grandkids, trying to 'make up for lost time'] have been the best six days of probably my whole life." "Immediately after making this statement," the narrator's plummy voice goes, "he realized that it was true."

Does Royal (Gene Hackman the great) ever *not* say precisely the wrong thing? He tells the kids at Margot's birthday party that the characters she's created "just weren't believable," were "just a bunch of little kids in animal costumes," but that that's "just one man's opinion." Words wound. Anderson's comic timing's perfect as the Happy Birthday song begins just as young Margot hands back the present Royal's given her and says "Goodnight, everyone." The hurt, incredulous look on her face says it all: her dad's a horrible person, remorseless, and furthermore he can't help it. What a lesson for all three Ten children to learn: significant grown-ups are nasty and don't seem to want to be otherwise. No wonder Chas, Richie, and

Margot collectively don't want to become one, an adult. Royal refers to Rachel, Chas's dead and still much-cherished wife, as "another body buried out there," in the cemetery; and consoles/informs Ari and Uzi that their "mother was a very attractive woman." That's his obituary to them, for them— the whole of it. He found his own daughter-in-law very attractive. Just like, when at the end of the film, as Richie professes his love for his own sister, Royal what-the-hecks, saying "she's a great-looking girl." Total scallywag.

Royal takes no pains to hide the fact that he "loves" Richie most, though he asks the Baumer, unfeelingly, "Why'd you choke out there that day, Baumer?" Not exactly personable, either, to refer to your own kid using his professional sports nickname, one that, now, only serves to remind Richie that he bombed out, that he's the kind of guy only old-timers and drifters in cemeteries are excited to (former) star sight. Even though he tells Chas the truth ("I think you're having a nervous breakdown. I don't think you've recovered from Rachel's death"), it's the brutal truth, and he's sarcastic with him, mocking, yelling back in the great scene in the closet with all the board games, all those symbols of childhood fun, stashed away now, retired like Royal is. He cheated on Etheline, he drinks a martini (royally served by the ever-faithful Pagoda) in front of the children as he fails to explain why they're separating, soft soaps his behavior by "acknowledging" he "wasn't as true to her" as he could have been. He makes excuses for the inexcusable. "I don't think you're an asshole," Mr. Sherman, the voice of authority, says at the film's conclusion, "I just think you're kind of a son of a bitch." "Thank you," Royal replies, much to our amusement, "genuine" gratitude and humility honeying his tone.

And yet even if he is unloving and unlovable, we the filmgoers love him. And Richie, a pacifying pacifist (who lost to a guy called "Gandhi" out there that legendary day at "Windswept Fields"), who doesn't want to compete any longer, just wants to live and let live and keep on being in love with Margot—Richie loves him. Just as he loves the equally obnoxious (as Royal—Chas is Royal's bona fide chip-off-the-old-block), unlovable, and unloving Chas:

CHAS—*Why do you hate me?*

RICHIE—*I don't hate you, Chas. You're my brother. I love you.*

CHAS—*Stop saying that!*

Lonely himself, Richie is the only one to see in his father what he sees in himself, the only one to recognize that Royal is "lonelier than he's ever been." Even if Royal's brought that on himself, it's no reason to shun him, Richie argues (for dad) in the meeting/caucus at Tenenbaum central. Just as Chas is angry and bitter, so is Richie sorrowful and sweet. These, the script warns, are the fruits of lovelessness and selfish parenting. And maybe indulgent parenting, too: Etheline lives for the kids, dotes on them, writes a book about them, *Family of Geniuses*, spoils them, gives her life over to them, and represses her own sexuality, presumably, for them—she hasn't, she tells Henry, "been with a man in eighteen years." A major case (a basket case and head case) of arrested development, Richie dresses the part, stuck in the bad past with his Björn Borg–issue headband and sweatbands that'll come in handy once he finally goes and slits his wrists. Just because *The Royal Tenenbaums* is a fairy tale doesn't mean it won't or can't face gruesome truths and unpleasant scenes, however aestheticized (the lurid bathroom suicide scene is red-beautiful). After all, the ur-fairy tale tellers, the Brothers Grimm, were super grim, too. Read the *real*, original "Cinderella" some time and see. Richie's artistic, but not an "artist" like his sister: he "failed to develop as an artist," Alec Baldwin's voiceover tells us. Yeah, well, if you only have one subject—your sister—and one genre (*portraits* of her, that Etheline mounts under Richie's direction rather than getting him the therapy he really needs), a regular Van Gogh you're not exactly going to turn out to be, though you can cut yourself like he did. Richie seems to give his life, or what's left of it, over to his sister. He reads a "Black Sparrow Press" edition of the pretentiously titled *Three Plays* by Margot Tenenbaum, and, jealously, he hurts himself when he learns from Raleigh St. Clair that she's having an affair. Even though he's traveled the world, he's seen nothing, it's meant nothing, he hasn't grown or learned how to be. He wants to come home and stay there, regress. He doesn't want to grow up. All three kids are, like Max and Blume, "little children." For now, that is.

Margot, a self-centered washout of a wife in perpetual fur coat (or in the bath, locked away, indulging in cigarettes and risking her life, the fan at the edge of the tub like some kind of Borderline Personality Disorder sufferer) is a mess, as well. "Why does he get to do that?" she whines as Ethel informs her that Chas and the boys have moved in. The self-reflexive posters for her plays scream pretentiousness and art-school dilettantism, shock for shock's sake. Anderson shoots her, in a mini-version of the same fur coat, reading hardbacks (more books for all us book lovers/bookworms) of Chekhov and Shaw—two artists that'd be way over the head of any kid, even a geniusy one. Her loss of a finger, in quest of her "real," not adopted, family, perpetually reminds her she's wounded, damaged, the artist-as-freak (accident), a curiosity with a prop smoke in her hand and tragic eyes, kohl-black. Margot's another Andersonian poser, along the lines of the punk pretenders the Ramones lampoon in Margot's make-out montage/theme song "Judy Was a Punk." The song is a perfect fit: for punk the genre was predicated on posing, on fakery and bravado-as-surrogate-for-talent or even proficiency at an instrument, despite what die-hard spike-haired experts might tell you backstage at the next punk rock gig you go to. You take a quick look at the Ramones' piss-take lyrics and you'll see the song makes fun of a punk and a runt (someone whose growth's been stunted) who do obligatory punk things and "perhaps they'll die," and therefore become legends like Sid and Nancy. Margot's an artist-imposter, all right; no wonder she narcissistically "falls" for a brief spell for another one: Eli Cash.

As Cash, Owen Wilson is great. Said to be a send-up of one of the greatest (of) American pretenders, Cormac McCarthy, Eli is a *complete and total* phony, like the ones Holden Caulfield rails against, like the thing old Holden railed against most: the movies and how they'll "ruin you." It's no coincidence that Anderson has Eli's on-air meltdown (if Richie had one, why can't would-be Tenenbaum he?) segue to an interview with another American charlatan: James Frey. Blink and you'll miss it, the Frey connection, in the scene where father Royal and daughter Margot watch black-and-white TV in the "hospital" room Royal rigs up at the house on Archer Avenue. Eli Cash is the kind of guy who thinks that an "artist" is a guy who does drugs, does *Wildcat* kinda stuff, wears an eccentric hat (symbol of identity), and has an affair with a femme fatale. Hollywood/Los Angeles is overrun with such creatures, people who think that they'll be taken seriously, taken for real artists, if only they act weird and say strange things. Even as he readies himself to bang Margot, he poses in the closet in his ridiculous hat, cocking his hip like a gunslinger/cocksman, clearly on some kind of drug, spaced out. The passage from his book, *Old Custer*, that he reads at the reading (just look at the public, the critics, fawning over the wrong guy— what gleeful revenge for Anderson, "neglected"

Anderson) is a great parody of the kind of obscure obfuscation and fustian that McCarthy and his ilk churn out with aplomb and to great plaudits, kudos, and applause, shit-eating-grinning all the way to the bank, presumably. Explaining the purport of his latest novel's ludic premise to trotting-fawning reporters, Eli can't even keep a straight face: "Everyone knows Custer died at Little Big Horn. What my book proposes is...maybe he didn't?" Classic Anderson. Post-event, Eli goes straight to the telephone, not to "the bank" to rack up more sales but to the emotional one, the emotional bank—for it all means nothing without Margot's approval, without her thinking he too is a genius: "You didn't even have to think about it," he says when in fishing for a compliment he lands instead a harsh truth: not only will he never be a genius, he'll never be a Tenenbaum. He'll be a wannabe Ten, so he may as well just try and sleep with one. He's a nerd-groupie, Eli—that strange Warholian thing: a famous guy who fawns over other "famous" people. Quel kook. "You never gave me the time of day till I started getting good reviews," Eli grouses in the break up scene with Margot. "Your reviews aren't that good," she says. "But the sales are," he parries. Touché. Telling. *Sales*: the all-American Dream/ scam redux. I don't want to quote the quote from the book within the book within the book because I don't want to support bad (fictional) "art" here and get you all curious about novels like *Blood Meridian* and *All the Pretty Horses* lest you go buy them or even check them out at the lending library—in case you haven't already. Many people have. *Many* people. What a *crap* culture we've constructed, bolstered, prizing celebrity over spirituality and the pursuit of inner peace, harmony, love for God, love for one another, all that good old stuff.

Sorry if you're a McCarthy fan. And/or a fan of Ben Stiller—churlish Chas. Most moviegoers have someone they love to hate, hate to love, an actor or actress whom they just can't stand. They don't know why, but they just *can't*. In his screaming red–for-alarm-and-danger Adidas track suit (one that'll turn Hamlet-mourning black, for Royal and for himself at the film's end), an egoist and egotist just like "Pappy," Chas fumes, jumps around, an ireful troll living in an attic on Archer Ave., not under a bridge. He comes "unglued" like Anderson likes, outraged and outrageous, a Napoleon in a home office, taking over a little world of finance, losing his soul and himself while he wins. He's hurting his kids just like Dad did. A walking avatar of how modern man is so afraid to lose that he forgets to live, to be. "To

be or not to be?" that is the question Chas makes a
mockery of: being *is* being in pain, and parading it
angrily. He runs psychotic fire drills in the middle of
the night that instill fear and paranoia in the boys,
"We're all dead," he announces. It's like he enjoys
being let down by them. He is like most people, no
extraordinary guy: he would rather be *right* than be
happy. Chas is that sad, urban-contemporary thing:
the walking dead, a self sacrificed to success, to
keeping up appearances and "market values." He's
a failure of a human being and he's a real piece of
work, not just unlovable and unloving but utterly
unlikeable, as well. He thinks he loves his boys, that
he's protecting them, but he's not. "Because you're
hurting me!" Royal yelps after Chas asks why he
should forgive the old man. Woe to those who
hurt the ones they "love" in the name of protecting
them. Chas's sibling rivalry with Richie is pathetic.
He can barely wave or say hello, from the window
above it all, as Richie comes home. "Who gives a
shit?" Chas says as Richie proposes that they let
Dad come home. "I do," Richie states, keeping it
simple like Anthony did. "You poor sucker," says
Chas, heartlessly, "you poor, washed-up papa's
boy." A "funny" line. "We like him," Ari or Uzi says.
"Pappy?" Chas ogres. "Let's not let this get out of
control," Mr. Sherman, an accountant calling Chas

to account for himself, prudently suggests. Too late: Chas has been out of control, we imagine, for years. Disgustedly, Chas, who is neither his brother's nor his father's keeper, turns round the poster (another *portrait*) of his brother on the tennis court, not wanting his kids to be reminded they even have an uncle (think back to Mr. Henry's warning to Future Man about waking up one day and finding you don't have a brother or even any friends; Chas has no friends). Chas needn't consider Margot a rival because, well, it's obvious that she's no competition at all when it comes to daddy's love and affection. "This is my adopted daughter," Royal introduces her, "Margot Tenenbaum." "Well, she wasn't your real grandmother," he counters when she tells us she's never been invited out to The Maddox Cemetery. Who *says* things like that? Only people who haven't become human yet, learned how and the way to be.

Another parody within this parody, another broken "person," is Raleigh St. Clair, Margot's uxorious and effete husband. Said to be based on the guy who wrote those tomes about a man mistaking his wife for a hat, Raleigh's a mandarinish fool who spends his days writing boffinish books on the indigenous peoples of "atolls" and doing foolish "experiments" on dunderheaded Dudleys—the antithesis of prodigies. Dudley is just a stupid kid, a dumb-dumb in a summer sun or fishing hat because his brain's on perpetual holiday. Yet Raleigh finds him fascinating: "How interesting, how bizarre!" What's Wes Anderson sending up here, with this particular set of puppets? Scientific fakirs and phonies and their quarry? Popular scientifics not mechanics? Hard to say. "How much do you already know?" the investigating detective asks. "Very little, I'm afraid," Raleigh says, about his wife's life, her affair, but the line could refer to how little academics like him know about the real world, and themselves. Or is it Raleigh is just an oddity/quiddity there because he can be, and because art is what "I" say it is, to paraphrase Magritte or Dali or one of those guys. Maybe it's part of Anderson's purport here that, prodigy or idiot, we're focusing on the wrong stuff, in art and in science and in the world at large. We're not paying attention to being, how to be, and expending our energies outside the self, everywhere else but internally. That's making Wes Anderson, I realize, into a saint or sage himself, but fuck it, "I'm building it anyway," that argument, to echo Max. "Isn't the true poet or painter a seer?" J. D. Salinger's Buddy Glass asks in the aforementioned *Seymour: An Introduction*. And what the seer sees is death.

And "death is the mother of beauty," as Wallace Stevens notes.

Death is redemption in this more "serious" film, and Royal can only go, expire, after he's been saved by himself and his awakening, his relinquishing of his "claim" on "my woman," and his atonement for his many sins (against everyone, including himself). Another Wes Anderson film, another antagonizing protagonist getting humiliated. "This is humiliating," Royal, barking about his encyclopedias being taken, "objects" (like the lawyer he used to be). "I want this family to love me," Royal (and rightly—and wrongly) confesses as Pagoda dresses *his* wound, one Pagoda's given him (*again!* Just like back in old Calcutta). Has *everybody* got a wound in this picture? Well, yeah. "It's your own damn fault, man," Pagoda, servant-sage, pronounces, administering oral medicine. Actions (and the action that failing to act inexorably is) have consequences, dire ones: look at Raleigh laid out on the couch in his "studio," devastated by Margot's sexual betrayal (I mean, what did he expect?) while dopey Dudley gormlessly tries to console him with the offer of more experiments. Sad sack songsmith Elliot Smith and his junky/suicide song "Needle in the Hay" provides the soundtrack for Richie's reaction/determination to kill himself. He's gonna top himself because his sister is cheating on his brother-in-law? Well, Richie's her "real" husband, yeah. Plus the intertextuality, as it were, of the characters' "stories" has never been anything less than internicene, surely.

The fake crisis that Royal occasioned is bookended by the real one that Richie prompts— for he survives his putative self-slaughter so that all Tens can rally around yet another hospital bed, this time for real. Even Chas seems affected, though he does seize the opportunity to sound like Royal: "Why'd you try to kill yourself?" Calamity leads to the truth, which could lead to reconciliation. In the waiting room, Margot cops to her infidelities, and her smoking. Maybe things'll work out all right. Cliché as it sounds, maybe the truth will set you free. Free to be who you should/need to be. Raleigh changes, too: he lights one up. "How long have you been a smoker?" Ethel asks her, as Anderson echoes Anderson in the bleacher scene with Max and Miss Cross. "Well, I think you should quit." We are *way* deep in Andersonland now. What a maze and haze of cross-references and in-jokes! A near infinite CinemaWorld for us to adventure around in. For what? Why? The question must be asked. To what end? Or does there have to be one? Nick Drake, patron saint of martyr-artists, sings about getting "second grace" as the bizarre scene unfolds and Richie, like a demented Anthony, breaks out of hospital and goes home, home to Margot and a camp-out just like the one they rigged up at the Natural History Museum. "I checked myself out," Richie puns. They compare wounds the way little kids would: "How many stiches did you get?" A gruesome sight. Happily, Margot's starting to feel for others, as well: "Poor Eli," she says when Richie brings him up. There's hope for her after all. Margot guesses, with another make-out scene that is somehow not prurient but chaste, sincere and sweetly sweet, that they'll have to be "secretly in love with each other" and leave it at that, for the rest of their lives. Cute as Max's quip about Rushmore. These are puppets becoming real characters, boy and girl Pinocchio's.

Royal's redemption commences as he does that very American/Andersonian thing: he gets a job. As an elevator *operator*, he learns to serve. Others this time, not himself. He hopes someone notices; he's trying to get recognition, but now in a good way, as a stand-up guy. On another rooftop, Richie and Royal have a heart-to-heart father-and-son as Mordecai comes back—the symbol of loss and childhood concerns returned. Redemption begets redemption as Richie tries to "save" Eli, take him to get some help. "I always wanted to *be* a Tenenbaum, you know," Eli says. "Me, too," Royal goes.

We, too, somehow.

Father-daughter ice cream—another ice cream, another reconciliation scene. There are many, many motifs, little self-referential touches throughout *The Royal Tenenbaums,* that I've left untouched, left for you, if you so desire, to puzzle out, loose ends for you to stitch together so that you can feel yourselves somewhat / somehow a part of the dazzling tapestries Anderson favors (both literal and literary), now that *my* themes have been limned, like the various instances of mise en abyme I've pointed out again and again.

A wedding scene for a happy ending, a car crash for drama, Chas learning Henry's "a widower" like himself (there's hope for him: he too might marry again, be happy, stop testily testing everyone), the death / sacrifice of Buckley the dog so that Royal can do another dadly thing and get the boys a new pet, a Dalmatian like the mice that Chas bred as a kid, a fight between zonked-out Eli and angry Chas, foaming at the mouth, a madman till he realizes what an asshole he is, but who hasn't got to actually thump anybody till now. "I need help," Eli admits, for real this time. "Me, too," Chas chimes in.

We, too, sometimes. On account of "they" say that asking for help—emotional/familial—is one of the hardest things for us to do.

Everybody thrives, but realistically. Margot's new play—she's reborn as an artist—gets "mixed reviews." For "mixed reviews," yet another self-reflexive nod, are surely what people who "used to be a genius" (as Royal says to Margot, upbraiding her unfairly) surely can expect: in light of the fact that their new work will always be compared to what they did earlier, when the ravenously curious and the professionally critical burned to see what all the fuss was about. For most, the post-prodigy work will pale in comparison. Obligatory "mixed reviews" are what boy-auteur Wes Andersons get, early on, until they're "understood" by the critics, welcomed to the canon instead of shot down for trying. Getting it greatly together, having fun now, Richie pays it forward at the preposterous "375th Street Y," coaches kids tennis, beautifully punishes a junior's shot with a model forehand and great follow-through, swatting it like the top pro he can't ever stop being, the killer instinct a professional athlete needs in order to compete—it's comfortingly there. The shot reminds us of Blume and the swat at the kiddie court—but a swat in a good way. Is that a *Prince* racket Richie's swinging? Ha! No matter. What counts is that Richie's engaged with the world again; he's not signing up for any sorry old cruise line anytime soon. Earlier we had a good laugh at his incredible "Meltdown!" (as the sensationalist sports mag, another text within the text, screams), but now we're maybe a bit choked up ourselves—to witness how far he's come since he choked "out there." He is, after all, our favorite Ten— next to Royal, of course.

Tragic chanteuse Nico serenades us home—to a cemetery. For the king must die, as we all must. Royal gets the epitaph/headstone engraving he's wanted and maybe deserved—a lie but an adorable one, about rescuing his family, at sea, from the *wreckage* of a *destroyer*. Which he has done, while saving himself.

This is a very great and very sentimental film— therefore, good *and* bad.

Like ourselves. Self-reflexively.

Author photo by Steve Keros

JOHN ANDREW FREDRICK was born in Richmond, Virginia, and grew up in Santa Barbara, California. After receiving his PhD from the University of California, Santa Barbara, he formed an indie rock band called **the black watch** that has released eighteen records to considerable acclaim. He lives in Los Angeles.